DATA GOVERNANCE

COLLECTION

I0013566

SEMANTICS AND POWER OF DATA

CONSISTENCY

GOVERNANCE

STANDARDIZATION

Prof. Marcus Vinicius Pinto - Marcão

ISBN: **9798314291627**

Publishing imprint: Independently published

Summary

1 Foreword.

Effective data governance requires a clear understanding of information semantics, as data only acquires real value when it is well defined, contextualized, and understood uniformly within an organization."

John Ladley[1]

We live in the age of massive data, where information permeates every aspect of society and business. However, what distinguishes raw data from actionable knowledge is semantics—the ability to give meaning, context, and intelligibility to information.

" Semantics and the Power of Data" is an essential book for those who wish not only to understand but also to apply semantic principles in data governance and information management.

This book is part of the Data Governance collection, a series that explores the essential components for building a solid foundation for management and artificial intelligence.

If you are a data scientist, information architect, IT manager, data governance specialist or professional involved in the structuring and quality of information within your organization, this book is written for you.

---

[1] John Ladley is an expert in data governance, information strategy, and knowledge management, with more than 30 years of experience helping organizations transform data into strategic assets. The author of influential books such as Data Governance: How to Design, Deploy, and Sustain an Effective Data Governance Program, Ladley is recognized for his hands-on, results-oriented approach to implementing data governance programs.

Professionals working with interoperability, metadata management, data dictionaries, big data, machine learning, and artificial intelligence will find here a fundamental guide to transforming disorganized data into structured, actionable knowledge.

The book presents key concepts such as semantic governance, informational standardization, differentiation between data, information, and knowledge, as well as the impact of semantics on interoperability and data modeling.

Fundamental technologies such as Linked Data, RDF, OWL, and SKOS are also explored, providing a comprehensive overview of the main tools for structuring meaning in informational ecosystems.

Reading this book not only broadens the theoretical understanding of information semantics but also offers practical insights and case studies that show how these approaches are being applied in different industries, such as healthcare, finance, government, and industry 4.0. With this, you will be prepared to face real challenges in information management and contribute to the evolution of data governance in your organization.

Learning about semantics is not only a competitive differential but an urgent need for professionals who want to work with data intelligently and strategically. Therefore, I invite you to explore this book and continue your journey by purchasing the other volumes of the Data Governance collection.

By understanding how to structure and interpret information accurately and effectively, you will be one step ahead in the data-driven economy revolution.

Welcome to this immersion in the universe of information semantics. Your journey to intelligent data management starts now.

Prof. Marcão - Marcus Vinícius Pinto

M.Sc. in Information Technology.
Consultant, Mentor, Speaker and Writer
on Information Technology topics,
Artificial Intelligence, Data Governance,
Information Architecture and Humanities.

2 Semantics as a Pillar of Governance and Information Quality.

Contemporary society witnesses the unquestionable rise of data as the new critical infrastructure for economic, political, and scientific decisions. In this scenario, data governance imposes itself as an epistemological and technical challenge, requiring a rigorous semantic architecture to ensure the intelligibility, interoperability, and reliability of information.

As stated by Floridi (2011) and Berners-Lee et al. (2001), the quality of information depends less on the volume of accumulated data and more on the semantic structuring that gives it meaning.

The semantics of data thus transcends mere technical standardization: it constitutes a strategic field of power in the global informational ecosystem. The absence of robust semantic criteria compromises the reliability of information and generates what Luciano Floridi calls "infossmog", that is, informational noise that distorts analyses and compromises critical decisions (FLORIDI, 2011). Semantics and Ontology: The Conceptual Architecture of Data.

Semantics, as a field of knowledge, studies the meaning and structure of the signs that allow communication and the transmission of information. In the context of data governance, this approach translates into the conceptual modeling of information through ontologies, taxonomies, and controlled vocabularies.

Data ontologies, as described by Guarino, Oberle and Staab (2009), constitute formal representations of knowledge, establishing semantic relationships between entities, attributes and concepts.

They play a key role in building knowledge bases, ensuring that data is interpretable in a consistent manner across different systems and agents.

Berners-Lee (2001) introduced this approach in the concept of Semantic Web, which advocates the creation of an environment in which data is readable not only by humans but also by machines, ensuring interoperability and efficient reuse of information.

The Resource Description Framework (RDF) and the Web Ontology Language (OWL) emerge in this context as fundamental standards for the representation of metadata and structured semantic relations (BERNERS-LEE et al., 2001).

The absence of well-defined ontologies and semantic rules results in what Peirce (1955) would call inconsistent interpretive abduction, i.e., a logic that fails to derive meanings, leading to misinterpretations and structural contradictions in the data. As such, data governance cannot be limited to technical compliance; it must incorporate semantics as a central axis in the organization of knowledge.

2.1   Semantic Governance and the Fight Against Informational Entropy.

Data governance has traditionally been concerned with integrity, security, and regulatory compliance. However, without a clear semantic structure, such efforts become insufficient. The concept of semantic governance, discussed by Yu and He (2016), refers to the need for strict management of the meanings attributed to data within an organization.

Semantic fragmentation – characterized by the coexistence of multiple definitions for the same concept – compromises informational consistency and increases data entropy. This dissonance generates concrete impacts, such as:

1. Inconsistency in analysis – different corporate departments can interpret the same data in different ways, compromising reports and forecasts.

2. Regulatory imprecision – semantic discrepancies make it difficult to comply with legislation such as GDPR and LGPD, which require clarity on the processing of personal data.

3. Operational inefficiency – the lack of semantic standardization reduces interoperability between systems, generating redundancies and increasing costs.

To mitigate such challenges, international organizations such as ISO/IEC 11179 and the FAIR Data Principles propose guidelines for the construction of structured metadata repositories, promoting transparency and semantic consistency (WILKINSON et al., 2016).

2.2   Semantic Standardization and Interoperability: From Chaos to Informational Order.

The complexity of modern data ecosystems demands robust semantic standards that ensure interoperability between different domains and applications. Semantic standardization is based on three essential principles:

1. Reuse of controlled vocabulary: the use of standards such as Dublin Core, schema.org and CIDOC CRM reduces ambiguities and facilitates data integration.

2. Formalization of semantic metadata: the implementation of well-defined ontologies ensures the uniform interpretation of information.

3. Adoption of persistent identifiers: technologies such as Linked Data and resolvable URIs allow the creation of interconnected semantic networks, expanding informational connectivity.

Semantic interoperability is not a technical luxury but a strategic imperative. Organizations such as the World Wide Web Consortium (W3C) have been promoting standards such as JSON-LD and SHACL to ensure semantic integrity in the digital environment (HEATH; BIZER, 2011).

2.3 Artificial Intelligence and the Evolution of Computational Semantics.

The rise of artificial intelligence redefines the role of semantics in data governance. The development of semantic agents, capable of inferring meanings and structuring data automatically, marks a new paradigm in information management.

Models such as BERT (Bidirectional Encoder Representations from Transformers), proposed by Devlin et al. (2018), demonstrate how neural networks can understand the semantic context of data, expanding the ability to categorize and analyze unstructured information.

The impact of this approach is reflected in applications such as:

- NLP (Natural Language Processing): extraction of meaning in corporate texts.

- Recommendation systems: personalization based on semantic inferences.

- Anomaly detection: Identifying inconsistent patterns in large volumes of data.

However, the advancement of semantic AI imposes new ethical and technical challenges, such as the risk of interpretative biases and the need for auditing mechanisms for algorithmic decisions (MITCHELL, 2019).

3 Differentiation between Data, Information and Knowledge: An Epistemological and Technological Approach.

The distinction between data, information, and knowledge is a central issue in epistemology and data governance. Although often used interchangeably in everyday discourse, these concepts have fundamental differences that directly influence the management, analysis, and use of the informational heritage of organizations and societies.

This distinction can be understood from different perspectives – philosophical, computational, and organizational – and has direct implications for the construction of data models, the quality of information, and the generation of strategic intelligence. As outlined by authors such as Ackoff (1989), Davenport and Prusak (1998) and Nonaka and Takeuchi (1995), the path from data to knowledge follows a logical and hierarchical progression, with profound implications for information science and semantic governance.

3.1 Data: The Raw Material of Knowledge.

Data constitutes the primordial basis of any informational structure. They are primary, raw elements, without an explicit interpretative structure. In essence, data is representations of facts, events, or transactions captured in their most elementary form, without any context or meaning assigned.

In the field of computing and data management, data can be numbers, texts, signs, or any form of symbolic representation stored in databases. Its main characteristic is semantic neutrality: an isolated number, a geographic coordinate or a set of characters does not, by themselves, carry intelligible meaning without a context of interpretation.

For example, consider the following raw data extracted from a temperature sensor:

23.4, 24.1, 25.0, 26.3, 27.8

Without an explicit reference, these numbers have no practical use. They need to be organized and contextualized so that they become information.

Key data features:

- Gross representation of events or phenomena.
- They have no inherent semantic interpretation.
- They are stored in structured or unstructured formats.
- They depend on processing to generate value.

3.2   Information: The Semantic Structuring of Data.

Data, when organized, contextualized and related, becomes information. Information is, therefore, a set of data that has been processed and acquired meaning within a given context.

Information not only describes facts but also establishes relationships between them, allowing for interpretation and decision-making. The transition from data to information occurs through processes of curation, organization, and contextualization.

Going back to the example of temperature data, structuring these numbers can generate a clear meaning:

Temperatures recorded (in °C) in the city of São Paulo during February 25, 2025:

08h: 23.4°C

12h: 24.1°C

4pm: 25.0°C

8pm: 26.3°C

00h: 27.8°C

Now, the raw data has been converted into information, as it is associated with a specific context: the thermal variation over the course of a day in a specific city.

Main characteristics of the information:

- It results from the processing and structuring of data.

- It has context and meaning within a specific domain.

- It allows inferences and comparisons but it does not yet constitute knowledge.

- It can be structured in tables, reports, dashboards, and graphs.

It is important to note that the information can be true or false. The quality of the information depends on the accuracy, reliability, and relevance of the data used in its construction. In data governance, processes such as data lineage and data quality are key to ensuring that the information derived is accurate and useful.

3.3   knowledge: The Critical Synthesis of Information.

Knowledge emerges when information is assimilated, interpreted, and internalized by individuals or intelligent systems. It represents the ability to understand patterns, make predictions, and make informed decisions.

While information answers the question 'What happened?', knowledge seeks to answer 'Why did it happen?' and 'What might happen next?'. It manifests in the form of theories, predictive models, heuristics, and expertise.

For example, a meteorologist may utilize historical temperature, humidity, and pressure information to predict future climate trends. At that time, the information was processed at a higher level of abstraction, becoming applied knowledge.

Nonaka and Takeuchi (1995) define organizational knowledge as a strategic asset that can be classified in two ways:

1. Tacit knowledge: intuitive, subjective and difficult to formalize, acquired through experience and practice.

2. Explicit knowledge: formalized and documented, and can be shared through manuals, reports, and computer models.

Main characteristics of knowledge:

- It goes beyond the simple possession of information, involving interpretation and application.
- It depends on the experience and cognition of the subject or system.
- It can be represented in heuristics, patterns, theories, and predictive models.
- It allows strategic decision-making and innovations.

The construction of knowledge is not linear. As Polanyi (1966) states, "we know more than we can express", emphasizing that much of human knowledge is tacit and difficult to be fully transferred to formal systems.

3.4   From Knowledge to Intelligence: The Highest Level of the Hierarchy.

If knowledge represents the ability to interpret and apply information, intelligence is the ability to formulate strategies, anticipate scenarios and adapt to new situations.

Intelligence can be understood as the dynamic use of knowledge to solve complex problems.

In the age of big data, the distinction between knowledge and intelligence becomes essential. The mere accumulation of large volumes of information does not imply organizational intelligence. A higher level of analysis is needed – through machine learning techniques, neural networks, and semantic models – to transform knowledge into effective strategic decision-making.

Davenport and Prusak (1998) point out that the great challenge of modern organizations is not to obtain data but to be able to convert it into a competitive advantage. Business intelligence is, therefore, a continuous process of extracting value from knowledge.

3.5   The Importance of Semantics in the Construction of Knowledge.

The distinction between data, information, and knowledge is not merely conceptual but rather a structuring axis of data governance and information science. The absence of well-defined semantic criteria prevents the efficient conversion of data into strategic insights.

In the age of artificial intelligence and cognitive systems, understanding this hierarchy becomes even more critical. Tools such as semantic ontologies, knowledge networks, and machine learning are essential to ensure that the information generated is intelligible and useful.

Semantic governance, therefore, is not just a technical issue but an epistemological strategy to transform informational chaos into competitive advantage.

4 The Impact of Semantics on Interoperability: From Fragmentation to Connected Intelligence.

Digital transformation and the exponential growth of data production have elevated interoperability to the status of an essential element for the efficiency of information systems.

Governments, corporations, and scientific institutions today operate in increasingly complex data ecosystems, in which the exchange of information between heterogeneous systems is critical for competitiveness and innovation.

However, interoperability is not limited to the technical capacity to exchange data. It requires robust semantic alignment that allows different systems to not only transfer information but understand it equivalently.

As highlighted by Berners-Lee, Hendler, and Lassila (2001), the Semantic Web aims at precisely this goal: to build an infrastructure in which machines and humans can process and interpret data in an interoperable and contextualized way.

4.1 Interoperability: Concept and Challenges in the Data Age.

Interoperability can be defined as the ability of different systems, devices, or organizations to share, process, and understand information efficiently and without loss of meaning (HEATH; BIZER, 2011).

In the context of data governance, interoperability is not restricted to technical connectivity; It must ensure that data transits with semantic fidelity, that is, that a concept expressed in one system is interpreted in an equivalent way in another.

The lack of semantic interoperability generates problems such as:

- Heterogeneity of data formats: systems use different standards, such as XML, JSON, and RDF, without a semantic mapping between them.

- Terminological ambiguity: Different domains use the same terms for different concepts or different terms for equivalent concepts.

- Lack of ontological alignment: absence of well-defined ontologies that establish relationships between concepts in different contexts.

- Regulatory and institutional barriers: Restrictions on data sharing due to divergent rules on privacy and compliance.

These challenges demand an approach based on semantic governance, which ensures a consistent layer of meaning on the data, promoting its interoperability.

4.2   The Role of Semantics in Interoperability: An Ontological Paradigm.

Information semantics cannot be dissociated from interoperability, as it is the layer responsible for ensuring that systems understand data in a coherent and uniform way. The ontological approach to semantic interoperability can be organized into three main levels:

Syntactic interoperability refers to the technical ability to exchange data, ensuring that systems can read and process files in structured formats such as CSV, XML, and JSON. However, this layer does not solve the problem of interpreting the meaning of the data.

On the other hand, semantic interoperability ensures that the information exchanged is interpreted correctly, regardless of the context of the sending and receiving system. As stated by Euzenat and Shvaiko (2013), semantic interoperability avoids knowledge fragmentation and promotes data convergence in heterogeneous ecosystems.

Ontologies are explicit formalizations of knowledge that establish hierarchical and semantic relationships between concepts. They are essential for interoperability because they allow disparate systems to share a common basis of meaning.

For example, in healthcare, the use of ontologies such as SNOMED CT (Systematized Nomenclature of Medicine – Clinical Terms) standardizes medical terminology across different hospital systems and electronic medical records. This structuring prevents the same clinical term from being interpreted differently in different hospitals, ensuring greater accuracy in diagnoses and treatments.

In addition, standards such as OWL (Web Ontology Language) and RDF (Resource Description Framework) enable the semantic modeling of data on the Web, creating interoperable knowledge networks.

4.3   Technologies and Standards for Semantic Interoperability.

Several standards and technologies have been developed to enable semantic interoperability in complex environments. Some of the key ones include:

4.3.1   Linked Data and Semantic Web.

The Linked Data approach, proposed by Berners-Lee (2006), promotes the publication of data on the Web using semantic patterns, allowing different systems to interpret and reuse information in a connected way.

This methodology is based on principles such as:

- Use of URIs to identify entities and concepts.

- Use of RDF to describe semantic relations.

- Adoption of controlled vocabularies, such as schema.org and FOAF.

This approach allows, for example, government, academic and business databases to interconnect without loss of meaning, promoting global data interoperability.

4.3.2 JSON-LD and SHACL.

To facilitate semantic integration between modern systems, formats such as JSON-LD (JSON for Linking Data), which incorporates semantic metadata into traditional JSON files, and SHACL (Shapes Constraint Language), which defines rules for semantic validation of data in RDF graphs, have been developed.

These technologies are widely used in e-commerce systems, social networks, and open data platforms, ensuring that information about products, user profiles, and events is understood uniformly by different services.

4.4   Use Cases: Semantic Interoperability in Practice.

The applicability of semantic interoperability can be observed in several sectors:

1   Digital Health and Electronic Medical Records.

Interoperability between hospital systems and public health networks is essential to ensure continuity of patient care.

The adoption of semantic standards, such as HL7 FHIR and LOINC, allows electronic medical records to be shared between different hospitals and laboratories, avoiding medical errors and redundancies in clinical examinations.

2   Public Data Governance.

Governments in several countries have been implementing semantic standards to ensure the transparency and interoperability of public data. The use of DCAT (Data Catalog Vocabulary), a semantic vocabulary for metadata, makes it possible for open data portals to be integrated globally.

3   Artificial Intelligence and Machine Learning.

AI models rely heavily on structured data to offer accurate predictions. Incorporating semantic ontologies improves the performance of machine learning systems, as it ensures that algorithms understand data at a deeper level, reducing interpretive biases.

4.5   Final Considerations.

Semantic interoperability is an imperative in the age of connected data. Without a solid semantic structure, information fragmentation leads to inefficiencies, ambiguities, and operational risks. The advancement of technologies such as Semantic Web, Linked Data, and ontologies points to a future in which data will not only transit between systems but will be understood accurately and consistently.

5 Fundamentals of Data and Metadata Modeling: Structures, Concepts and Governance.

Data modeling is one of the pillars of information management, being essential to structure, organize, and make data available in an efficient and consistent way. In a scenario where data production grows exponentially – driven by technologies such as Big Data, Artificial Intelligence and the Internet of Things (IoT) – the need for structured modeling becomes even more pressing.

The effectiveness of data modeling lies not only in the definition of relational schemas or the organization of tables and columns but also in the ability to ensure semantic meaning and interoperability. In this context, metadata plays a crucial role in providing information about the structure, provenance, and context of data, ensuring that its use is reliable and replicable.

5.1 Data Modeling: Fundamental Concepts.

Data modeling can be defined as the process of creating structured representations of information, establishing rules and relationships between different entities to allow efficient data manipulation. This process is essential for building robust databases, data warehouses, and analytic architecture.

Data modeling can be analyzed under three main levels:

1 Conceptual Modeling.

Conceptual modeling represents data in an abstract way, focusing on identifying the main entities and their relationships. This model is technology-agnostic and is used to establish a common vocabulary among different stakeholders within an organization.

Widely used tools and methodologies include:

- Entity-relationship diagrams (DER) (CHEN, 1976): graphical representation of entities and their attributes.

- Ontological models: define formal and logical semantics between concepts, allowing interoperability between distinct domains (GUARINO; OBERLE; STAAB, 2009).

- Semantic frameworks: such as RDF and OWL, which allow semantic representation of data on the Web (BERNERS-LEE, 2001).

Conceptual modeling facilitates communication between technical and executive teams, ensuring that the data structure reflects business objectives.

2   Logic Modeling.

Logical modeling details the structure of data based on a specific model, defining tables, columns, primary and foreign keys, normalizations, and integrity constraints.

Different logic modeling paradigms include:

- Relational models: based on set theory and widely used in databases such as PostgreSQL, Oracle, and SQL Server (Codd, 1970).

- Graph models: used to represent complex networks, being used in recommendation and social intelligence systems (ANGLES; GUTIÉRREZ, 2008).

- NoSQL models: Applicable to distributed, scalable systems, such as MongoDB and Cassandra, where schema flexibility is prioritized.

Logical modeling allows business rules to be translated into implementable structures in computer systems.

3   Physical Modeling.

Physical modeling describes the implementation of logical models in database management systems (DBMS). This level involves optimizing performance, indexes, partitions, and storage tuning.

Factors such as data distribution, security, and scalability are critical in physical modeling, especially in Big Data and cloud computing environments (STONEBRAKER, 2010).

5.2   Metadata: Information Governance.

If data modeling defines the structure of information, metadata ensures its interpretation and traceability. Metadata is often described as "data about data," but this simplistic definition fails to capture its complexity and importance in information governance.

5.2.1   Types of Metadata.

Metadata is classified into three main categories:

- Descriptive metadata: Provides information about the content and meaning of the data. Examples include titles, descriptions, keywords, and categories.

- Structural metadata: Defines the relationship between different data and your organization. A classic example is database schemas and XML standards.

- Administrative metadata: contains information about provenance, access, and legal restrictions, and is essential for compliance with regulations such as LGPD and GDPR.

5.2.2   Metadata Standards.

Standardizing metadata is essential for interoperability and consistency in information governance.

Key standards include:

- Dublin Core (DCMI): One of the most widely used standards for metadata cataloging on the Web.

- ISO/IEC 11179: international standard for metadata governance in corporate systems.

- FAIR Data Principles: principles that promote findability, accessibility, interoperability and reuse of data (WILKINSON et al., 2016).

The use of standards allows metadata to ensure the auditability, traceability, and reproducibility of data.

5.2.3   The Intersection of Data Modeling and Metadata in Information Governance.

Effective data governance depends on the integration between data modeling and metadata. Without a robust metadata framework, data modeling becomes vulnerable to inconsistencies, redundancies, and loss of meaning.

Best practices include:

- Data Cataloging: implementation of data dictionaries to document the structure and semantics of information.

- Data Lineage: traceability of the data lifecycle, ensuring transparency and reliability.

- Metadata Automation: use of machine learning for automatic metadata extraction and enrichment.

Aligning data modeling and metadata makes it possible to create more resilient information architectures, allowing organizations to maximize the value of their data assets.

5.3   Reflections on the Evolution of Modeling and Metadata.

Data modeling and metadata are not just technical tools; they are essential strategies for managing informational complexity. With the emergence of data lakes, artificial intelligence, and semantic automation, new challenges arise in data modeling, requiring increasingly sophisticated approaches.

The construction of intelligent semantic models, aligned with ontologies and global standards, will be the difference between organizations that dominate their data and those that become hostages of informational chaos.

6 Ontologies and Taxonomies: Building a Shared Vocabulary in Data Governance

The exponential growth in data production and consumption has posed significant challenges for the organization, integration and reuse of knowledge in different domains. With the proliferation of heterogeneous databases, semantic fragmentation has become a critical problem, hindering interoperability between systems and compromising the quality of information.

In this context, the construction of a shared vocabulary through ontologies and taxonomies has become essential to ensure semantic consistency, interoperability, and efficient data governance. While taxonomies structure concepts into hierarchical classifications, ontologies formalize relationships and semantic rules, allowing systems and human agents to understand data in a uniform way.

6.1   The Problem of Semantic Fragmentation and the Importance of Controlled Vocabularies.

Semantic fragmentation occurs when different systems or organizations use inconsistent or divergent terminologies to describe similar concepts. This problem directly impacts data interoperability, generating challenges such as:

- Terminological inconsistency: The same entity can be named in different ways in different contexts (e.g., "customer," "consumer," "user").

- Semantic ambiguity: the same term can take on different meanings in different domains (e.g., "bank" can mean "financial institution" or "seat").

- Lack of interoperability: the absence of semantic standardization prevents the integration of databases and the automation of processes based on machine learning.

The adoption of controlled vocabularies – organized sets of standardized terms and definitions – reduces semantic fragmentation and facilitates communication between different systems and actors. The two main instruments for the construction of controlled vocabulary are taxonomies and ontologies.

6.2   Taxonomies: Hierarchical Classification of Concepts.

Taxonomies organize concepts in a hierarchical manner, grouping terms according to well-defined categories and subcategories. This structuring is essential for the efficient cataloging and retrieval of information, and is widely used in digital libraries, knowledge bases, and document management systems.

Characteristics of Taxonomies:

- Hierarchical structure: Concepts are organized in a parent-child relationship (e.g., "Vehicles" → "Cars" → "Sedans").

- Focus on classification: The primary goal is to categorize entities in a structured schema.

- Semantic simplicity: Relationships are primarily hierarchical, without the logical complexity present in ontologies.

Examples of Applied Taxonomies:

- Dewey decimal classification (DDC): a book classification system used in libraries.

- Taxonomy of the Organization for Economic Cooperation and Development (OECD): standardized classification of economic sectors.

- E-commerce category hierarchy: Structures used in marketplaces like Amazon and eBay to organize products.

Despite their usefulness, taxonomies have limitations, as they do not capture more complex semantic relationships, such as equivalence, causality, or dependence between concepts. For more sophisticated modeling, ontologies are needed.

6.3   Ontologies: Formalizing Relations and Meanings.

Unlike taxonomies, which are limited to hierarchical classification, ontologies provide a richer semantic structure, defining relationships, constraints, and properties between concepts.

According to Gruber (1993), ontologies are "explicit and formal specifications of a shared conceptualization", allowing different agents (humans or machines) to interpret and process data in a consistent manner.

The adoption of ontologies allows the creation of structured and semantically consistent knowledge bases.

Some examples include:

- Semantic Web: Use of RDF, OWL, and SPARQL to Model Interconnected Data on the Web (BERNERS-LEE, 2001).

- Biomedical ontologies: Gene Ontology (GO) structures genetic information for scientific research.

- Interoperability between corporate databases: Ontologies ensure that different sectors of an organization share the same understanding of customers, products, and processes.

The main advantage of ontologies over taxonomies is their ability to infer: ontological-based systems can generate new knowledge automatically, through computational logical reasoning.

Fundamental Elements of Ontology:

- Concepts (classes or categories): represent entities in the domain (example: "Person", "Product", "City").

- Relationships (properties or predicates): define associations between concepts (example: "Customer buys Product").

- Axioms and logical rules: constrain or infer new relationships between entities (e.g., "Every employee must belong to a department").

- Instances (individuals): These are concrete examples of classes (e.g., "John is an instance of the Person class").

Application of Ontologies in Data Governance.

6.4   Building a Shared Vocabulary: Good Practices.

Building an effective shared vocabulary requires strategic planning that aligns organizational objectives with well-defined semantic patterns. Some best practices include:

- Adopt recognized standards: The use of vocabulary such as schema.org, SKOS, FOAF, and Dublin Core improves interoperability.

- Use modeling tools: Software such as Protégé, TopBraid Composer, and OntoUML make it easy to create robust ontologies.

- Create an institutional glossary: documenting the key terms used in the organization avoids ambiguity and redundancies.

- Promote semantic governance: periodically update and revise taxonomies and ontologies to reflect changes in the domain of knowledge.

6.5   Reflections on the Future of Ontologies and Taxonomies

The convergence between artificial intelligence, Semantic Web, and big data is transforming the way ontologies and taxonomies are developed and applied.

The advancement of semantic neural networks and knowledge-based machine learning suggests that in the future, ontologies could be self-actualizing and integrated with AI systems to ensure the dynamic evolution of shared vocabularies.

The massive adoption of Linked Data and Knowledge Graphs will consolidate ontologies as the foundation for global data interoperability, driving innovations in information governance and strategic decision-making.

7 Metadata Standards: Dublin Core, RDF, OWL, and SKOS in Data Governance.

The growing digitalization of production processes and the explosion in the volume of data demand new strategies to ensure the organization, retrieval, interoperability and governance of information. In this context, metadata plays a central role in providing structured descriptions of the data, allowing disparate systems to exchange information in a consistent manner.

However, for metadata to fulfill its function effectively, it is essential that it follows well-defined semantic standards, ensuring that data descriptions are understood and interpreted uniformly across different domains and applications.

Among the main metadata standards used globally, the Dublin Core (DCMI), Resource Description Framework (RDF), Web Ontology Language (OWL) and Simple Knowledge Organization System (SKOS) stand out.

7.1 Metadata and the Need for Structured Standards.

Metadata can be defined as "data about data" – that is, structured information that describes both digital and non-digital resources. They provide context for the data, allowing organization, cataloging, retrieval, and preservation of information over time.

The absence of standardization in metadata creation can lead to semantic fragmentation, hindering interoperability between systems and generating inconsistencies in the way data is interpreted and reused.

To mitigate these challenges, standards have been developed that ensure semantic uniformity, promoting findability, accessibility, interoperability, and reuse of data – principles known as FAIR Data Principles (WILKINSON et al., 2016).

Key standards adopted globally include:

- Dublin Core (DCMI): A simplified set of descriptive metadata widely used for cataloging and indexing digital and physical documents.

- Resource Description Framework (RDF): a fundamental model for the representation of metadata in the Semantic Web, allowing the creation of knowledge graphs.

- Web Ontology Language (OWL): An ontological modeling standard that expands the capabilities of RDF by enabling inferences and advanced logical representation.

- Simple Knowledge Organization System (SKOS): a model for structured representation of taxonomies, thesaurus, and controlled vocabularies.

Each of these standards has specificities that make them suitable for different contexts and applications, as will be detailed below.

7.1.1   Dublin Core: The Simple and Universal Basis for Descriptive Metadata.

The Dublin Core Metadata Initiative (DCMI) was developed in the 1990s as a basic set of metadata to describe digital and physical resources. The model is widely adopted due to its simplicity, flexibility, and compatibility with various domains (WEIBLE, 2003).

The Dublin Core standard defines 15 fundamental elements for describing a feature, including:

- Title: Name assigned to the resource.

- Creator: entity responsible for creating the resource.

- Subject: main theme of the appeal.

- Description: summary of the content.

- Publisher: entity responsible for making the resource available.

- Date: Date associated with the resource.

- Type: Category of the asset (text, image, audio, etc.).

In addition, Dublin Core Qualified adds refinements to increase the accuracy of the description, allowing for greater semantic control.

Dublin Core Applications:

- Cataloguing digital documents in digital libraries and institutional repositories.

- Indexing of academic and scientific content.

- Organization of metadata in government and open data portals.

While Dublin Core is a widely accepted standard, its simple, generalist structure may be insufficient for more complex domains. For advanced applications on the Semantic Web, more robust standards such as RDF and OWL are required.

7.1.2   RDF: Structuring Metadata on the Semantic Web

The Resource Description Framework (RDF) is a foundational model for representing metadata in a structured way on the web. Developed by the World Wide Web Consortium (W3C), RDF allows data to be interconnected and interpreted in a consistent manner, enabling the construction of semantic graphs (HEATH; BIZER, 2011).

The RDF adopts a model based on triples, where each unit of information is represented in the form:

Subject → Predicate → Object

Example:

<https://exemplo.com/pessoa/joao> <foaf:name> "John Smith".

This means that John Doe (subject) has a noun (predicate) equal to "John Doe" (object). This approach allows data to be connected in a global semantic network.

RDF Applications:

- Representation of interconnected data on the Semantic Web.

- Construction of knowledge graphs, such as Wikidata and Google Knowledge Graph.

- Data modeling in Linked Data and Open Data.

Despite its flexibility, RDF does not define logical rules or inferences, requiring the use of more advanced standards, such as OWL.

7.1.3   OWL: Ontological Modeling for Semantic Inferences.

The Web Ontology Language (OWL) expands the capabilities of RDF, allowing the creation of formal ontologies, with the definition of classes, properties and advanced logical rules (GUARINO et al., 2009).

OWL introduces concepts such as:

- Classes and subclasses: Example: "Doctor" is a subclass of "Health Professional".

- Logical relations: definition of equivalences, constraints, and cardinalities.

- Semantic inferences: Allows machines to deduce new information automatically.

- OWL Applications:

- Development of biomedical and scientific ontologies.

- Structuring of knowledge bases in AI.

- Semantic interoperability in complex enterprise systems.

7.1.4   SKOS: Structuring Vocabularies and Taxonomies.

The Simple Knowledge Organization System (SKOS) is a standard developed to represent taxonomies, thesaurus, and controlled vocabularies in a structured way (MILES; BECHHOFER, 2009).

Features of SKOS:

- Defines hierarchical terms and relationships.

- It allows mapping between different vocabularies.

- Facilitates semantic integration between knowledge bases.

Applications of SKOS:

- Representation of scientific and technical classifications.

- Modeling of business taxonomies.

- Construction of a thesaurus for information retrieval.

7.2   Future of Metadata Standards.

The convergence between Semantic Web, Linked Data, and Artificial Intelligence requires the continuous advancement of metadata standards.

Emerging technologies such as knowledge graphs and semantic automation will transform the way data is organized and interpreted.

8 Semantic Standardization and Normalization: Ensuring Data Consistency and Interoperability.

The accelerated growth in data production and consumption has brought with it a critical problem for organizations and information systems: semantic fragmentation and data inconsistency. Different industries, domains, and applications use different terminologies, formats, and standards, making integration and interoperability between systems a significant challenge.

Semantic standardization and normalization emerge as essential strategies to ensure that data is interpretable, reusable, and efficiently integrated. By establishing clear rules of nomenclature, structuring, and harmonization, semantic standardization ensures that disparate systems share the same understanding of the concepts represented in the data.

8.1 Principles of Standardization and Harmonization of Data.

Semantic normalization aims to reduce ambiguities and inconsistencies in data, ensuring that different systems can use it in a uniform and structured way. This process involves:

- Definition of a standardized semantic model. Establish a schema of metadata and shared ontologies to represent entities, attributes, and relationships.

- Terminological alignment. Create a controlled vocabulary to avoid conflicting synonyms and ambiguous terms.

- Persistent identification of data. Use unique, resolvable identifiers, such as Uniform Resource Identifiers (URIs), to reference entities.

- Harmonization of data formats and schemas. Adopt interoperable standards such as JSON-LD, RDF, OWL, and SKOS to ensure compatibility between heterogeneous databases.

2.1. Benefits of Semantic Normalization

Applying these principles has a number of benefits for organizations and data systems:

- Improvement in data quality: reduction of redundancies, errors and inconsistencies.

- Interoperability between systems: Facilitated integration between corporate, government, and academic databases.

- Data process automation: easy implementation of data pipelines for ETL (Extract, Transform, Load) and machine learning.

- Efficiency in analysis and decision-making: standardized data enables more accurate and reliable insights.

8.1.1   Rules of Nomenclature and Data Structuring.

The adoption of standardized rules for naming and structuring data is an essential component of semantic governance. The lack of uniform criteria for naming and organizing data can lead to misinterpretations and hinder interoperability.

Key guidelines for data naming and structuring include:

- Consistency in the choice of terms: use controlled vocabulary and avoid conflicting synonyms.

- Use of naming standards: Adopt conventions such as camelCase, snake_case, or kebab-case to ensure readability and compatibility.

- Avoid ambiguous abbreviations: Abbreviations should be standardized and documented to avoid misinterpretation.

- Incorporate semantic context: Attribute names should clearly indicate the meaning of the data represented.

Example of a standardized structure for naming attributes in a relational database:

Field Name	Meaning	Value Example
client_name	Customer's full name	John Doe
date_birth	Date of birth	20/06/1985
code_order	Order identifier	ORD12345

In addition to nomenclature, the way data is organized and structured has a direct impact on interoperability and reuse.

Some guidelines include:

- Use of normalized schemas: application of data normalization techniques to avoid redundancies and ensure integrity.

- Adoption of metadata standards: use of Dublin Core, DCAT and ISO 11179 to describe and catalog data.

- Standardization of exchange formats: Preference for JSON-LD, XML, standardized CSV, and RDF to facilitate integration between systems.

The correct structuring of data ensures that its semantics are preserved throughout the entire informational lifecycle, reducing operational risks and improving the governance of information assets.

8.2   Case Studies: Global Semantic Standardization Initiatives.

Several initiatives around the world have promoted standardization and semantic normalization to ensure interoperability and data quality. Below, we highlight three examples of successful cases in the implementation of semantic governance.

8.2.1 Open Data Standards: The European Union Experience.

The European Union has been leading the adoption of open data standards, ensuring that government information is accessible and interoperable across different countries.

- The Data Catalog Vocabulary Application Profile (DCAT-AP) has been adopted as the standard for metadata of public data portals.

- The European Interoperability Framework (EIF) initiative establishes guidelines for semantic integration between different nations.

- The use of persistent URIs and Linked Data has facilitated the interconnectivity of government data.

This model served as a reference for open data initiatives in several countries, including Brazil, Canada, and Australia.

8.2.2 Gene Ontology: Semantic Standardization in Biomedical Research.

In the field of biomedicine, Gene Ontology (GO) is one of the most successful examples of standardized ontology for the description of genetic data.

- It allows researchers around the world to use a unified terminology to describe gene functions.

- It uses OWL and RDF for semantic modeling, ensuring compatibility with AI systems.

- Its hierarchical structure enables advanced semantic inferences.

The success of the GO demonstrates the impact of semantic standardization on science, enabling global collaboration and accelerating biomedical discoveries.

8.2.3   Schema.org and Web Interoperability.

Schema.org is a collaborative initiative between Google, Microsoft, Yahoo! and others to define standardized vocabulary for the Web.

- Uses JSON-LD and RDFa to structure metadata in web pages.
- It facilitates indexing and retrieval of data by search engines.
- It allows the creation of rich snippets and knowledge graphs, improving the user experience.

The adoption of Schema.org has been instrumental in improving the quality of data on the web, making it more understandable by machines and semantic agents.

8.3   The Future of Semantic Standardization.

Semantic standardization and normalization are critical elements for data governance, artificial intelligence, and the Semantic Web. As the complexity of information ecosystems grows, semantic alignment between different domains becomes a competitive differentiator.

The implementation of dynamic ontologies, interoperability standards, and automated data governance promises to take semantic standardization to a new level, enabling the creation of increasingly integrated and intelligent data ecosystems.

9 Data Dictionaries and Metadata Catalogs: Structuring and Governance for Information Quality

The increasing complexity of data ecosystems requires formal documentation and organization mechanisms to ensure the quality, traceability, and interoperability of information. Without a clear structure, organizations face challenges such as inconsistent data, semantic redundancy, and difficulties in integrating heterogeneous systems.

In this scenario, data dictionaries and metadata catalogs play a key role in information governance, ensuring that data is clearly documented, versioned, and accessible to different teams and processes.

9.1 What is a Data Dictionary?

Data dictionaries are structured repositories that document the data elements used in a system, providing information about their definition, format, type, relationships, and constraints.

A well-structured data dictionary not only defines the attributes of a database but also establishes a common vocabulary for both technical and business users, avoiding ambiguity and inconsistencies in the manipulation of the data.

The use of data dictionaries is essential to ensure:

- Semantic consistency: Sets standards for data naming and structure, minimizing ambiguity.

- Interoperability: facilitates integration between heterogeneous systems by ensuring a standardized vocabulary.

- Data quality: reduces redundancies and inconsistencies by establishing clear validation and relationship rules between entities.

- Governance and compliance: supports audits, change tracking, and compliance with regulations such as LGPD, GDPR, and ISO/IEC 11179.

9.2   Structuring a Data Dictionary.

Data dictionaries can be structured in a variety of ways, depending on the context and application domain. They usually include the following elements:

Attribute	Description	Example
Field Name	Unique attribute identifier	cliente_nome
Description	Explanation of the attribute's meaning	"Customer's full name"
Type of Data	Stored Value Type	VARCHAR (100)
Restrictions	Integrity rules (PK, FK, NOT NULL etc	NOT NULL
Relationships	Connections to other tables or entities	Customers → orders

In addition to this information, more sophisticated data dictionaries can include validation rules, modification histories, and semantic classifications to broaden their use in data governance processes.

Why keep an up-to-date Data Dictionary?

- Clarity and consistency: facilitates the understanding of the terms used, avoiding ambiguity.

- Onboarding new members: New developers can quickly become familiar with the system.

- Efficient maintenance: in case of maintenance or upgrades to the system, having an updated dictionary makes it easier to identify and change specific components.

- Decision documentation: helps to understand the history and logic behind certain architectural choices.

How to create an effective Data Dictionary?

- Start early: The dictionary should be started at the beginning of the project and updated continuously.

- Be detailed: Each entry should include not only the name of the identifier but also its description, data type, input restrictions, and any relevant context information.

- Easy to consult: organize the dictionary in a logical way, whether alphabetically, by category or by system, so that information can be found quickly.

- Use tools: Documentation software or code management platforms, such as Confluence or Git, can offer specific functionality to keep data dictionaries organized and accessible.

- Promote documentation governance: Establish clear policies on who can add, modify, or remove dictionary entries, ensuring that information remains accurate and current.

Examples and Best Practices.

Imagine you're working on a software project called "Secure Finance." In the context of this project, the term "transaction" is used on a recurring basis. In the data dictionary, you might have:

- Transaction (Transact): A financial operation executed by the user, which can be an expense or income. Attributes include transact_id (int, unique), transact_type (string, possible values: 'expense', 'income'), transact_amount (float), and transact_date (date).

Note that every aspect of the "transaction" is clearly defined, which reduces the chance of confusion. You could even include code examples or SQL queries that use the term.

Tips to Keep Updated:

- Regular revisions: Set a schedule of periodic revisions of the dictionary to ensure that it is up to date.

- Continuous integration: If possible, integrate the data dictionary into your development environment so that code updates automatically reflect it.

- User feedback: Encourage team members to provide feedback and suggest improvements to the dictionary.

- Versioning: Keep previous versions of the dictionary for reference and to document the evolution of the system.

9.2.1   Be Mindful of Business Conventions.

How effectively a team executes its information technology projects is often influenced by the clarity of communication between its members and other stakeholders.

One area where this mutual understanding is vital is the scope of naming conventions within documentation and system development.

Therefore, having naming conventions aligned with the organization's business processes is a practice that not only facilitates understanding and collaboration between the technical team and business users but also strengthens the company's cohesion and overall strategy.

Adequacy of nomenclatures to business processes:

- Intuitive understanding: When technical terms reflect the terminology used in business processes, business users can better understand the system's functionalities and the reports generated. For example, if a company refers to product delivery as "fulfillment," then the system and its documentation should also use that term consistently.

- Facilitation of training: New employees, especially those with previous experience in other industries or functions, can adapt more quickly if the nomenclatures are aligned with those practiced daily in the company's business.

- Better decision-making: Business analysts and managers could make informed decisions more efficiently if the nomenclature used in the system's data and reports matches the language used in their daily operations and strategies.

Tips for establishing effective naming conventions.

- Conduct alignment workshops: organize work sessions between the technical team and business users to discuss and agree on the terminologies to be used.

- Create a Naming Standards Document: Document and distribute the agreed-upon conventions so that they serve as a reference for the entire organization.

- Send naming surveys and feedback: Survey frequent users of systems and collect feedback on the effectiveness of current nomenclatures, adjusting where necessary.

- Foster a culture of awareness of the terms: Incorporate naming conventions into training and internal communication materials to reinforce their use and importance.

- Leverage term mapping tools: Implement tools that link technical and business terms in a dynamic, accessible, and updatable data dictionary.

When misaligned nomenclatures create barriers.

Let's look at a practical example: a financial organization internally uses the term "Premium Customer" to classify customers with high turnovers. In the absence of alignment, developers create information systems that refer to these customers as "Gold Customers."

It is easy to see how such divergence can lead to confusion, misinterpretation, and a need for constant translation between the concepts of the system and those used in business operations.

Consequences of Not Aligning Nomenclatures:

- Lack of consistency: Discrepancies in the terms used can cause inconsistencies in reporting and analysis.

- Slow adoption: Users may resist using new systems if the terms are incompatible, slowing down the adoption and implementation processes.

- Ineffective communication: The dialogue between technical and business teams can become complex and inefficient.

Example of Effective Practice.

To make this alignment a reality, imagine a business process called "Complaint Management". If business teams use terms such as "Complaint Ticket," "Customer Response," and "Incident Resolution," those same terms should be reflected in the systems.

This would entail labeling form fields, reports, and even code snippets with those specific terms. Adopting these terms would foster greater mutual understanding between the teams involved, from development to customer service.

The nomenclatures should, as far as possible, align with terminologies used in the organization's business processes. This ensures that business and technical users are on the same page.

10. Plan identifiers with scalability.

Think long-term and how the tags will behave with system expansions. Avoid names that may become obsolete or inappropriate as the system grows and evolves.

9.3   Metadata Catalogs: Structuring and Management Tools.

Metadata catalogs are centralized repositories that organize and document Metadata from different data sources, providing insight into the source, structure, meaning, and lifecycle of data.

Unlike data dictionaries, which focus on specific database attributes, Metadata catalogs act as global repositories, allowing for the indexing, crawling, and discovery of information across multiple systems.

A well-structured metadata catalog should contain:

- Technical metadata: information about structure, format, data types, and tables.

- Semantic metadata: definitions and meanings of data elements, ensuring terminological consistency.

- Administrative metadata: information on data governance, access control, and versioning.

- Data Lineage: record of the origin, transformations, and use of data throughout its lifecycle.

Implementing metadata catalogs improves efficiency in data discovery and reuse, ensuring transparency and governance.

9.4   Tools and Frameworks for Metadata Management.

Several tools and frameworks are used to manage and automate the control of metadata and data dictionaries. Some of the key solutions include:

Several tools and frameworks are used to manage and automate the control of metadata and data dictionaries.

Some of the main solutions available stand out:

- Apache Atlas: Metadata governance platform focused on Big Data ecosystems. Enables cataloging and tracking of the data lifecycle in distributed architectures such as Hadoop and Spark.

- Collibra Data Governance: an enterprise solution that enables cataloging and metadata management, offering functionalities for data governance, regulatory compliance, and automated information discovery.

- Alation: data catalog platform that uses machine learning to promote active metadata governance. Supports collaboration between users and facilitates the discovery of information within organizations.

- DataHub: open-source metadata catalog, developed by LinkedIn, that offers a scalable approach to capturing and indexing information in modern data ecosystems.

- Google Data Catalog: Metadata discovery and governance service in the cloud, integrated into the Google Cloud ecosystem. Allows you to catalog and organize data assets stored in services such as BigQuery, Cloud Storage, and Pub/Sub.

- Microsoft Purview: Microsoft's data governance platform, designed for enterprises that require centralized control and regulatory compliance. It supports data lineage, policy management, and automated metadata cataloging.

These tools play an essential role in automated documentation, data discovery, and usage auditing, ensuring compliance with regulations and governance standards, as well as improving efficiency and quality in data lifecycle management.

9.5   Metadata Governance and Versioning.

Metadata governance is essential to ensure traceability, compliance, and control over information in enterprise environments.

Principles of Metadata Governance:

- 1. Metadata Catalog centralization: unified storage of data descriptions in an accessible repository.

- 2. Versioning and Change History: traceability of metadata modifications to ensure auditing and compliance.

- 3. Access Control and Security: definition of permission policies and protection of sensitive data.

- 4. Governance Automation: implementation of automated processes for capturing and maintaining metadata.

5.2. Versioning of Metadata.

Metadata versioning allows you to track changes in data over time, ensuring reproducibility and regulatory compliance.

Common techniques include:

- Using Git for Structured Metadata: Versioning schemas and metadata definitions.

- Time-stamping and change logs: automatic recording of modifications to active metadata systems.

- Periodic metadata audits: continuous monitoring to ensure the quality and integrity of documented information.

9.6   The Future of Metadata Management.

With the advancement of artificial intelligence and semantic automation, metadata governance will become increasingly integrated into machine learning and predictive analytics processes. The use of knowledge graphs and data fabrics will allow a more efficient organization of metadata, reducing manual efforts and improving the quality of information.

Companies and institutions that adopt robust metadata catalogs and advanced governance strategies will be better prepared to face challenges related to interoperability, compliance, and data intelligence.

10 Semantic Component.

The notion of semantic components are fundamental in the creation of information systems, especially in the coherent naming of entities, attributes, and other constructions within a database or a computer system.

A semantic component is a basic unit of meaning within a language or system, which contributes to the understanding or interpretation of a more complex expression.

In the context of information systems and databases, a semantic component can be a complete word, an acronym, or an abbreviation that provides clear insights into the function, type, or content of a variable, attribute, or data element.

For example, in a database system, the term "customer" may be a semantic component used to identify an entity that represents people or companies that do business with an organization. This component helps infer the type of information you can expect to find associated with that entity, such as "Customer Name," "Customer Address," and "Customer Phone."

The semantic components are carefully chosen during the data modeling process to ensure that they are intuitively understandable and reflect the reality of the domain to which they refer. This helps in efficient communication between the users of the system, whether they are technical or not, and ensures that there is less chance of ambiguity or misunderstandings about the nature of the data one is working with.

A semantic component carries within itself the meaning necessary to convey what a particular word or symbol represents within the context of the system.

For example, in the naming of a database attribute for "Date of Birth", the choice of the words 'Date' and 'Birth' describes in a direct and understandable way the type of information that the attribute intends to store.

A word, in its use as a semantic component, is chosen for its ability to clearly communicate a specific idea or concept.

10.1   Short-form.

A short form acts as a condensed version of one or more words, usually in the form of an abbreviation or acronym, maintaining communication efficiency while saving space and effort.

For example, "CPF" is a widely recognized short form in Brazil to refer to the "Cadastro de Pessoas Físicas", a piece of information that is used to uniquely identify a Brazilian citizen. Similarly, "ID" is a common short form for "Identification" or "Identifier".

It is important that these abbreviations and acronyms are standard and recognizable by the users of the system to ensure that the communication of information is effective. In environments where short forms are used, they are commonly documented in a glossary or data dictionary, ensuring that everyone who interacts with the system shares the same understanding.

Thus, both full words and short forms are semantic compounds vital in the composition of names in data structures, each playing its role in promoting clarity, efficiency, and accuracy in the representation of information within information systems.

For example, in the naming of a database attribute for "Date of Birth", the choice of the words 'Date' and 'Birth' describes in a direct and understandable way the type of information that the attribute intends to store.

Similarly, a short form acts as a condensed version of one or more words, usually in the form of an abbreviation or acronym, maintaining communication efficiency while saving space and effort.

For example, "CPF" is a widely recognized short form in Brazil to refer to the "Cadastro de Pessoas Físicas", a piece of information that is used to uniquely identify a Brazilian citizen. Similarly, "ID" is a common short form for "Identification" or "Identifier".

It is important that these abbreviations and acronyms are standard and recognizable by the users of the system to ensure that the communication of information is effective. In environments where short forms are used, they are commonly documented in a glossary or data dictionary, ensuring that everyone who interacts with the system shares the same understanding.

Thus, both full words and short forms are semantic compounds vital in the composition of names in data structures, each playing its role in promoting clarity, efficiency, and accuracy in the representation of information within information systems.

There are two types of short shapes.

10.1.1 Natural short-forms.

Natural short-forms are, as the name suggests, abbreviations or acronyms that originate outside structured data systems but which gain acceptance and current use in everyday life. These short forms are created in the general scope of language and communication and can come from various sources, such as corporate language, technical jargon, legislation, or even popular usage.

Common examples are: IPI (Tax on Industrialized Products), PIS (Social Integration Program), ICMS (Tax on the Circulation of Goods and Services), CPF (Individual Taxpayer Registration) and IPTU (Urban Property and Land Tax) perfectly illustrate this concept.

These acronyms refer to technical and legal terms that are widely used in the Brazilian context, specifically in the fiscal and legal sphere, and are recognized by the general population, as well as by professionals from various areas.

In terms of a data dictionary or database, these natural short-forms are adopted without the need for additional definitions, due to their broad understanding and recognition. They provide a concise way to represent concepts that would otherwise require longer and more complex descriptions.

The adoption of these short-forms in a corporate data dictionary or information system facilitates communication and understanding between users and system developers.

However, it is important that they are used consistently and that their interpretation is unambiguous within the context in which they are applied, to avoid ambiguity or misunderstanding.

10.1.2 Derived short-forms.

Derived short-forms are abbreviations specifically designed to condense longer terms into shorter versions, making them easier to use in systems where space is an important consideration, such as user interfaces, programming, or data modeling.

These abbreviations are created from a defined portion of the characters of the original word, often the first four characters, or through a significant combination of letters that capture the essence of the full term.

This shortening is done out of practical necessity: it helps to maintain legibility and efficiency without losing the essential meaning. For example, "POST" immediately captures the root of the term "postal," implying actions or services related to the post or mail.

"DEVI", reduced from "due", can be used in financial or reporting contexts to represent outstanding amounts or obligations.

"EMIT", derived from "issued", is common in accounting and documentation contexts, suggesting the idea of generating or releasing documents, invoices, and the like.

"DSVT" can be used to indicate the concept of "development", whether in the context of design, software, or urban planning, for example.

Using derived short forms requires special care to ensure that the abbreviation created remains intuitive and is not confused with other terms that may have the same or similar reduction.

In addition, it is important that they are documented and standardized within the environment in which they are used, ensuring that all users of the system understand what each short-form represents. This is often done through a data dictionary or other type of reference documentation.

Thus, by creating and adopting derived abbreviations, organizations optimize the exchange of information and the operation of systems, although the creation and adoption of these should be done with due consideration for context and clarity of communication.

11 Types of Semantic Components.

The semantic components are organized into 4 types: identification, reference, qualification, and sentence.

11.1 Identification.

Identification, in the context of information systems and data modeling, involves the judicious combination of words and short forms, whether natural or derived, with the aim of creating unique and meaningful identifiers for data elements.

These identifiers perform the dual function of distinguishing one element of data from others and clearly conveying the meaning or context of that element.

For example, in a customer management system, a data field might be labeled "CustomerPrimaryEmail." This identifier is the concatenation of the "Email", "Primary" and "Customer" components. "Email" suggests the type of data (an e-mail address), "Primary" indicates that, among several possible, this is the primary address, and "Customer" explicitly associates this data with the relevant entity in the system, which is the customer.

Together, these components fulfill the semantic and functional requirement of identification, assisting users and systems in locating and understanding data.

Identifiers are fundamental in the structuring of databases and computer systems, as they facilitate the organization, search and manipulation of data. They are also essential for maintaining data integrity, allowing complex systems to function efficiently and support decision-making based on accurate and well-defined information.

Effective identification of elements in data systems is essential to ensure clear, organized and accessible information management. Whether defining variables in a software program or naming fields in a database, there are several tips and recommended patterns that can improve the semantic and technical quality of these identifications.

The following are some guidelines to guide this process.

11.1.1   Use consistent nomenclatures.

The adoption of consistent nomenclatures is a fundamental point in the development of information systems and in the maintenance of databases. This consistency not only facilitates understanding and teamwork but also contributes to the development of more organized and maintainable software.

1.   Choose a Naming Convention.

Before you start coding or designing a database, it's vital to choose a naming convention. CamelCase, PascalCase, and snake_case are the most common:

- camelCase: The first letter is lowercase, and the first letters of subsequent words are uppercase, as in 'customerbirthdate'.

- PascalCase: identical to camelCase but the first letter is also uppercase, such as 'CustomerBirthDate'.

- snake_case: All words are written in lowercase and separated by underscores, as in 'data_nascimento_cliente'.

2.   System-Wide Consistency.

Once you've selected your preferred convention, apply it consistently across all variables, tables, and attributes. For example, if you choose camelCase for variable names, use it throughout your source code without exceptions.

3.   Document your choice.

Include your chosen naming convention in your project documentation, as well as in your guidelines for team contributions. This ensures that any new addition to the code or database maintains the established consistency.

4. Advantages of Consistency.

- Readability: consistently named code and data are easier to read and comprehend.

- Maintenance: it's easier to search, update, and manage information when you follow a unified convention.

- Collaboration: new team members or external collaborators can quickly get used to the system, due to the predictability of nomenclatures.

- Development Tools: many IDEs (Integrated Development Environments) and code analysis tools support naming conventions and can help maintain consistency.

Maintaining consistent nomenclatures is indicative of good practice and reflects a high standard of professionalism in software engineering and data management.

Disregarding consistency can lead to a cluttered system, where a lack of standard becomes a source of errors and inefficiencies.

Therefore, identify the standard that best fits your project, team, and business context, and firmly adopt it at all stages of development.

11.1.2 Be Descriptive but Concise.

The art of naming identifiers in a data system lies in the balance between descriptiveness and conciseness. Well-crafted identifiers should communicate the function or content of a variable or field clearly, without forcing the user to decipher an excessively long or complex name.

Here are some tips for achieving this balance:

- Prioritize clarity: the name should be immediately understandable to someone familiar with the context. Superfluous details that do not contribute to understanding should be avoided.

- Avoid obscure jargon and acronyms: unless an acronym is widely recognized in the context of usage, full words are preferable to avoid confusion.

- Use relevant keywords: include words that are essential to understanding what the field represents. For example, "CustomerEmail" clearly communicates that the field contains the customer's email address.

- Avoid redundancies: don't repeat the entity name or other words that are already implied in the context. For example, within a "Customer" table, simply "email" may suffice instead of "customeremail".

- Keep a reasonable length: a good goal is to keep names within the range of 8-20 characters if possible. Longer names are harder to read, especially on interfaces with limited space.

- Use complete words where it makes sense: there may be a temptation to shorten words to be more concise but this can obscure the meaning. "DataNasc" is less clear than "BirthDate", although it is shorter.

- Examples of good identifiers:
  - ✓ For a field that stores the last updated date of a record, use something like 'ultimoUpdate' or 'dataUltimaAtu'.
  - ✓ For a variable that calculates the total of an order, prefer 'OrderTotal' instead of 'OrderCalculatedTotalValue'.

Keep in mind that the way identifiers will be used also plays a role in how they should be named.

In an internal application where users are used to certain business terms, it may be acceptable to use more technical forms. In a consumer-facing application, clarity and simplicity are paramount.

Choosing identifiers that achieve the duality between being descriptive and concise requires careful consideration of the most critical aspects of the data or function being represented.

Doing this well is a skill that improves code readability, makes it easier for team members to understand, and supports efficiency and effectiveness in maintaining the system.

11.1.3 Avoid obscure abbreviations.

Abbreviations are often used to save space and facilitate written communication. However, it is important to keep in mind that some abbreviations may be obscure, i.e., little known or understood by readers. To avoid confusion and ensure clear communication, it is recommended to avoid using obscure abbreviations.

When possible, it is preferable to use full word forms or standardized abbreviations that are widely recognized. For example, instead of using the abbreviation "Num." for "Number," it is more advisable to write the full word, as this abbreviation may not be easily understood by all readers. Likewise, it is preferable to use established and known abbreviations, such as "CPF" for "Cadastro de Pessoa Física".

Here are some examples to illustrate the importance of avoiding obscure abbreviations:

Example 1:

- Wrong: The bkg of the report will be generated automatically.

- Correct: The background of the report will be generated automatically.

In this case, the abbreviation "bkg" may not be widely known, which can lead to confusion and make it difficult to understand the text. By using the full form of the word, "background", the meaning becomes clearer to all readers.

Example 2:

- Wrong: I need 2 un of product A.
- Correct: I need 2 units of product A.

Again, the abbreviation "un" is little known and can lead to confusion. By using the full form of the word, "units", the possibility of misinterpretation is avoided.

Example 3:

- Wrong: Please send the report w/ the data f/ analysis.
- Correct: Please send the report with the data for analysis.

In this example, the abbreviations "w/" and "f/" may not be easily understood by all readers. Using the full forms of the words, "with" and "for", the meaning of the sentence becomes clearer.

Therefore, when writing texts—whether in professional, academic, or personal documents—it is essential to avoid using obscure abbreviations. Instead, opt for full forms or standardized, widely recognized abbreviations. This ensures clear and objective communication, making it easier for readers to understand. Remember, clarity in writing is crucial for conveying information effectively.

While abbreviations can save space, they can be confusing if not widely recognized. If possible, prefer full forms or standardized abbreviations that are common knowledge, such as 'Id', 'Num' for 'Number', or established acronyms such as 'CPF'.

11.1.4 Use Prefixes and Suffixes When Appropriate.

Using prefixes and suffixes appropriately can bring clarity and organization to the naming of data and structures. Prefixes are added at the beginning of the name and can indicate the type of data, while suffixes are added at the end and can indicate the structure.

A common example of a prefix is the use of the prefix "is" to indicate Boolean values. For example, we can have the variable "isActive" to represent whether a customer is active or inactive. This prefix helps identify that the data is a Boolean condition, making it easier to understand the code.

Similarly, suffixes can be used to indicate the structure or purpose of an element. For example, in a database, it is common to add the suffix "Table" at the end of table names.

Thus, we could have the "CustomerTable" table to represent the table that stores the customer data. This convention helps to quickly identify the purpose of the structure.

However, it is important to utilize these prefixes and suffixes consistently and sparingly. Too many prefixes and suffixes can make names too long and confusing. In addition, it is necessary to consider the best practices and conventions adopted by the development community in which you are inserted.

Here are some examples to illustrate the appropriate use of prefixes and suffixes:

Example 1:

- Prefix: "is"
  - Variable: isActive
  - Meaning: Indicates whether the client is active (true) or inactive (false).

Example 2:

- Suffix: "Table"

  o Table: CustomerTable

  o Meaning: Represents the table that stores customer data.

Example 3:

- Prefix: "num"

  o Variable: numItems

  o Meaning: Indicates the number of items present in a list or set.

Example 4:

- Suffix: "List"

  o Structure: Products List

  o Meaning: Represents a list that stores the products.

Remember that the use of prefixes and suffixes must be done in accordance with the conventions adopted in your area of expertise. It's important to consult the best practices and guidelines established by the development community you're a part of.

Also, keep in mind that the clarity and readability of the code are key. Avoid excessive abbreviations or prefixes/suffixes that can make names too long and complex. The main goal is to make code easier to understand and maintain, making it more intuitive and cohesive.

By using prefixes and suffixes appropriately, you'll contribute to the organization and readability of your code. This makes teamwork easier, makes maintenance easier, and reduces the time it takes to understand and modify code.

11.1.5 Maintain proper specificity.

Maintaining proper specificity is essential to ensure clarity and accuracy in the communication of data or systems. It is important to adopt a level of specificity that corresponds to the complexity of the data or system in question.

When we refer to data or systems, it is common for there to be different elements with similar names but which perform different functions. To avoid confusion, it is recommended to identify each element specifically, indicating its function or purpose.

For example, if a system has multiple "dates" associated with different events, it is important to identify each of them in a specific way. We can have "CreationDate" to represent the creation date of an object or event, "UpdateDate" to show the date of the last update performed, among other possibilities. This way, it is clear to users or developers what the purpose of each specific date is.

Here are some examples to illustrate the importance of proper specificity:

Example 1:

- Variable: price
    - o Inadequate level of specificity: "price"
    - o Best level of specificity: "productprice" or "salesprice"

In this case, the name of the variable "price" is too generic and can lead to misinterpretations. It is recommended to add greater specificity, indicating whether it is the price of a specific product or the selling price, for example.

Example 2:

- Table: Data
    - o Inadequate level of specificity: "data"

- o Best level of specificity: "customerdata" or "requestInformation"

When using a table called "data," it can be difficult to identify its specific purpose or content. Adding a higher level of specificity, such as "customerdata" or "requestdata," helps clarify and make it easier for other developers to understand.

Proper specificity contributes to the clarity and organization of data and systems. This is critical to facilitate maintenance, understanding, and collaboration among team members, as well as to avoid potential confusion or misinterpretation.

However, it is important to strike a balance in the specificity of the names. Avoid being overly specific to the point of making names too long and complex. The specificity should be sufficient to clearly identify the data or system in question, but it should also be concise and legible.

By maintaining proper specificity, you will be contributing to the organization and understanding of the data or systems. This makes it easier to work as a team, maintain, and evolve projects.

Keep in mind that best practices may vary depending on the context and conventions adopted by the development community in which you are embedded. Referring to the guidelines and standards adopted by your team or community can be helpful in ensuring consistency and consistency in naming.

11.1.6 Avoid Numbers in Identifiers.

The careful use of numbers in identifiers is an important issue in information systems design. Although at first glance it may seem convenient to use numbers to differentiate similar elements, this practice can lead to confusion and difficulties in understanding and maintaining the system in the long term.

When it comes to creating identifiers, whether it's naming variables in programming code, fields in a database, or labels in a management system, clarity and expressiveness are essential.

For example, consider a database that stores information about vehicles. Using an identifier such as "Car1", "Car2", "Car3" for different records does not offer any indication about the specific characteristics of each vehicle. In addition to the lack of clarity, these identifiers become problematic when there is a need to enter more information or perform searches in the database. How to distinguish these vehicles without examining the details associated with each of them?

In contrast, adopting identifiers such as "CompactCar", "SUVLuxo" and "Pickup Truck" offers an immediate description of the type of vehicle and facilitates identification and access by users of the system.

From the description, it is possible to infer characteristics such as size, style and perhaps even the price range of the vehicle, without having to resort to detailed information. This is particularly useful in systems where users may not be technically familiar with the data, such as in a publicly accessible online catalog.

Another scenario in which numbers can be problematic is in the nomenclature of software versions. Identifiers such as "Version1", "Version2", "Version3" are common, but they do not communicate changes between versions. Terms such as "InitialVersion", "PerformanceImprovementVersion", "UpdatedInterfaceVersion" provide a more immediate meaning and help users understand the evolution of the software.

Additionally, when numbers are applied to identifiers without a clear context, they can quickly become obsolete or misleading due to changes in the system.

For example, if an identifier such as "MeetingRoom5" is used because it is the fifth room registered in the system, what happens if a room is removed? The numbering becomes discontinuous, and "MeetingRoom5" may no longer be the fifth room in the sequence, creating the potential for confusion.

The practice of using descriptive words instead of numbers also has immense value for the accessibility and internationalization of systems. Numerical identifiers can be ambiguous in different cultures and languages, while descriptive words can be more easily translated or adapted to local contexts, expanding the understanding and usability of the system.

Therefore, preferring words that describe the purpose or fundamental characteristic of an identifier is undoubtedly a recommended standard in computer science and data modeling. This approach not only improves the readability and maintainability of systems but also promotes a more intuitive and immediate understanding of data, which is critical for good user experience and operational efficiency.

11.1.7   Adopt Word Formation Patterns.

Adopting word formation standards is critical to maintaining consistency and organization across systems and projects. Considering the global scale and the predominance of English as a programming language, it is recommended to use English for identifiers in international systems.

By using English as a basis for identifiers, possible communication barriers between developers from different countries are avoided. This makes it easier to understand and collaborate on, making code more accessible and expanding the possibilities for sharing and reusing resources.

Additionally, it is important to establish clear rules for the formation of new terms, especially when it comes to compound words or technical names. These rules may include the use of separators, such as the use of initial capital letters in each word, or the use of hyphens to separate compound terms. Consistently choosing and applying these rules helps maintain the readability and clear identification of the identifiers used in the code.

Here are some examples of word formation patterns:

Example 1:

- Information System
- Identifier: informationSystem

In this example, we can use the first letter of each word as a capital letter to make it easier to read, without the need for separators between words.

Example 2:

- User identification code
- Identifier: userID or userId

In this case, the use of initial capital letters in each word (camel case) makes it easier to read and identify the identifier.

Example 3:

- Type of tax document
- Identifier: fiscalDocumentType

In this example, the words are concatenated and the first letter of each is capitalized, creating a clear and readable identifier.

When adopting word formation standards, it is important to consider the conventions adopted by the development community to which you belong. Refer to the guidelines and standards defined for the programming language or development environment used. This ensures

In global-scale systems, consider using English for identifiers, as it is the dominant programming language. Also, establish rules for the formation of new terms when working with compound words or technical names.

In any technological project, whether it's creating an app, implementing an information system, or developing a website, documentation plays a critical role. It ensures that all team members, current and future, can understand what was done, how it was done, and why certain design decisions were made.

11.1.8 Avoid Words with Ambiguous Semantic Load.

In systems development, one of the biggest challenges is to create a design that not only meets current needs but is also flexible enough to adapt to future growth and change.

This flexibility begins by planning identifiers – such as variable names, database tables, and other code nomenclatures – that play a critical role in the maintenance and expansion of software systems.

Thinking in the long term is essential, as identifiers must be robust enough to maintain their relevance and adequacy in the face of future expansions and evolutions of the system.

Tips for creating identifiers with scalability:

- Use of generic but descriptive nomenclatures. Choose names that clearly describe the function or object but aren't so specific that they become obsolete if there are changes in functionality. For example, prefer 'userProfile' to 'fiveFieldUserProfile', as the number of fields can vary.

- Avoid references to specific technologies. Names like 'ajaxLoader' may lose their meaning if AJAX technology is replaced in the future. A more enduring and technologically agnostic name could be 'dataLoader'.

- Use prefixes and suffixes with caution. Including data type or location information, such as 'strName' for a string or 'dbPassword' for a password in the database, may not be the best choice if these types or locations are susceptible to change.

- Flexible naming standards. Implement a naming system that can accommodate expansion without getting confused. Using patterns such as camelCase or snake_case can help maintain consistency without limiting growth.

- Avoid sequential numbers without context. Identifiers such as 'report1', 'report2', 'report3', etc., are uninformative and can lead to confusion. Instead of numbering sequentially, opt for qualifiers that describe the purpose of each report, such as 'annualReport', 'salesReport', 'customerFeedbackReport'.

- Focus on business mastery. Identifiers should reflect the domain of the business rather than abstract implementation ideas. For example, 'paymentGateway' is preferable to 'externalVendorService3'.

- Preparation for internationalization. If there is a possibility that the system will expand to different markets, consider using identifiers that are easily translatable or understood in multiple languages.

- Use high-level naming conventions. In complex systems, conventions that evidence the function in the system as a whole are useful, for example, 'auth' for authentication modules or 'svc' for services.

Examples of Planning with Scalability:

- An e-commerce system initially names a database table that stores item information as 'bookDetails'.

- However, when planning identifiers with scalability in mind, it is realized that e-commerce can, in the future, sell not only books but also a wide range of products. Therefore, a more suitable name would be 'productDetails', preparing the system for future inventory expansion without the need to rename the table, which would save resources and decrease the margin for error.

Practical Implementation of Scalable Identifiers.

In implementation, scalable identifiers must be accompanied by equally adaptable documentation.

Code versioning tools like Git and submodules help track changes to identifiers over time, while dynamic documentation systems allow for quick and efficient updates.

Challenges of Not Planning with Scalability.

Without a plan focused on scalability, the system may encounter several obstacles in the future, such as high costs to refactor the code base, difficulty in integrating new functions, and problems with readability and maintenance of the code.

Additionally, a system with outdated or insufficient nomenclatures can be less intuitive for new developers, increasing the time it takes them to become familiar and productive.

11.1.9 Reuse established identifiers.

Within the scope of systems development and software project maintenance, there is a fundamental practice that can bring numerous benefits: the reuse of established identifiers.

This approach not only creates a sense of familiarity and continuity throughout the organization but it also promotes a smoother learning curve, makes code easier to maintain, and avoids unnecessary increased complexity.

Advantages of Identifier Reuse:

- Facilitation of understanding. New systems or modules that employ familiar identifiers are more quickly understood by team members, regardless of their level of experience.

- Continuity of documentation. Existing documentation for a given identifier may continue to be relevant and useful even as new systems are implemented.

- Reduction of ambiguities. It avoids the proliferation of similar terms with slightly different meanings, which could confuse users and developers.

- Consistency in business processes. Using the same identifiers across different systems helps maintain consistency of business processes that are carried out across multiple platforms.

- Systems Integration. It facilitates integration between old and new systems, as data maps naturally and intuitively from one system to another.

Identifier Reuse Example:

- "declaracao_rendimento" in "declaracao_rendimentos_modelo_2". When expanding the system to include a new income statement template, the essence of the identifier is maintained ("declaracao_rendimento"), only adding a suffix that indicates the variation ("modelo_2"). This clarifies that it is an alternative version or type of the original statement but maintains the terminological basis already known.

- "company" in "empresa_compradora". Here, a generic identifier such as "company" is specialized to reflect a specific role in the context of the application – in this case, an entity making the purchase. This extension of the identifier preserves the common root while still providing clarity on the entity's role within the system.

- "document" in "documento_emitido". Similar to the previous example, "documento_emitido" is a specification of the more generic term "document", indicating that it is a particular subcategory or state of documents within the system, in this case, those that have been issued.

Tips for Effectively Reusing Identifiers:

- "Context analysis: Make sure that the identifier is relevant in the new context and that reuse does not confuse or dilute its original meaning.

- "Consistent naming standards: If you introduce a new suffix or prefix to distinguish variations of the original identifier, be consistent in applying that standard throughout the system.

- "Versioning of identifiers: when modifiers are added, such as "modelo_2", keep a clear track of the different versions and their applications within the system documentation.

- "Collaboration with stakeholders: Work closely with all stakeholders, including end users and technical team members, to ensure that the reuse of identifiers is beneficial to all.

11.2   Reference.

Referencing systems and databases plays a critical role in promoting consistency and understanding through the reuse of nomenclatures.

When a specific data element, such as a variable or a column name, has well-understood and established semantics, it can be referenced or repurposed to identify new elements in distinct but related contexts.

This helps maintain semantic integrity and makes it easier for technical teams and end users to interpret the data, especially in organizational structures where the elements have an intrinsic relationship.

Exploring the concept of Reference.

When you use the reference, you inherit the semantic meaning of an already established term, thus creating a direct link between different data sets that share a common context or attribute.

This method is effective in avoiding ambiguity and in strengthening the clarity of data within an organization.

Benefits of Referencing Identifiers:

- Semantic consistency: consistency of term interpretation is maintained across different systems and modules, simplifying data understanding and management.

- Ease of data integration: the unification of nomenclature facilitates the integration between different databases, systems or modules by ensuring that the same semantics are shared.

- Simplified documentation: documentation becomes less complex as the referenced terms are already described and defined elsewhere, reducing unnecessary duplication.

- Traceability: allows you to trace the origin of data and understand the relationships between different entities and attributes within the company's systems and processes.

Implementing Reference Effectively:

- Identify key elements. The first step is to identify which data elements have a strong identification and understanding within the company and that, therefore, could act as a basis for future references.

- Standardization. It is important that the referenced nomenclature follows pre-established standards, ensuring that the reference is made in a consistent manner.

- Context Evaluation. Before reusing an identifier, always evaluate whether the semantics of the term are applicable in the new context to avoid confusion.

- Keep the documentation up to date. Always update data documentation to include clear descriptions of how and where identifiers are referenced in new contexts.

- Training and Communication. Be sure to offer proper training to teams and effectively communicate naming conventions to avoid misunderstandings.

Cautions When Using Reference:

- Semantic Overload. Care must be taken not to overload a term with multiple meanings that can become confusing when applied in diverse contexts.

- Naming Conflicts. In large and complex systems, ensuring that the referenced nomenclature does not conflict with other identifiers is vital.

- Organizational Changes. Always consider how changes to business processes could affect the validity of referenced terms and be prepared to adjust as needed.

The Qualification Process:

- Identify contexts: determine the various contexts in which an identifier is or will be used.

- Specify properties: add properties to the identifier that describe its unique and distinct characteristics.

- Univocality: Continue the specification until the identifier becomes uniquely distinguishable.

- Avoid Excesses: ensure that the qualification does not make the identifier unnecessarily long or complex, maintaining the balance between specificity and simplicity.

When eligibility is optional. While qualification can add clarity, it can be optional for several reasons:

- Context sufficiency: if the context in which the identifier is used is sufficiently specific, additional qualifications may be unnecessary.

- Established conventions: in certain domains, there are conventions that already sufficiently establish the meaning of an identifier, making additional qualifications redundant.

- Inherent clarity: if the data element in question already has a clear descriptive name and the system is designed with an architecture that avoids ambiguity, the qualification may be superfluous.

Best Practices for Qualifying Identifiers:

- Relevance. Make sure that each qualifier you add offers a valuable and relevant distinction.

- Conciseness and Simplicity. Avoid qualifications that make identifiers wordy or complicated beyond necessity.

- Consistency. Adopt standard qualifications within the system to avoid confusion and facilitate maintenance.

- Documentation. Document the qualifiers used and their rationale to ensure that any team member can understand and follow the reasoning behind the nomenclature.

- Evolution of the System. Consider how future changes to the system may affect the relevance of your chosen qualifiers, and plan accordingly.

Qualification is undoubtedly a valuable tool in information systems design. It not only improves semantic accuracy but also increases data reliability and integrity over time.

However, it is essential that the qualification is implemented with prudence and justification, ensuring that it brings benefits in terms of

11.3   Sentence.

In data element nomenclature, the "sentence" is the mechanism employed to capture and transmit an action or functionality represented by a particular piece of data or process.

Sentence-based identifiers present a dynamic approach, often used to clarify not only the nature of a data entity but also the active role it plays in an operational context or system.

How Identifiers with Sentences Work:

The use of a verb, often in conjunction with a subject and/or complement, creates a sentence that assigns an explicit action to the identifier.

This practice is particularly useful in systems where processes or relationships need to be clearly defined by name, not just to describe a static entity but to highlight the interactions between different entities or actions in which they are involved.

Key Benefits of Identifiers with Sentences:

- Clarity in Actions. The sentence identifier provides immediate clarity of the activity or process represented by the data element, making it easier for users to understand the system's operations.

- Intuition in Processes. It reinforces intuitive understanding of business processes as it mirrors the way operations are discussed and understood in the real world.

- Self-explanatory. Improves system self-documentation; Identifiers that are descriptive phrases can reduce the need for additional references to understand the role of a data element.

How to Implement Sentence Identifiers Effectively.

- Clear Subject and Object. Include the subject and object, if applicable, to provide full context. Make sure they are related in a logical and understandable way.

- Grammatical consistency. Maintain grammatical consistency and adopt a standardized structure, such as always using the 3rd person singular or infinitive.

- Avoid ambiguity. Ensure that the identifier is unambiguous and that the action described can be clearly associated with the data element in question.

- Business and Technique Aligned. Work collaboratively with business and technical teams to ensure that sentence identifiers are relevant and understandable to all stakeholders.

Points of Consideration When Using Sentence Identifiers.

- System Complexity. Evaluate whether the use of sentences as identifiers unnecessarily increases complexity or effectively contributes to the clarity of the system.

- Internationalization. Think about how these identifiers can translate into multilingual environments. Sentences can be more difficult to translate or adapt for non-speakers of the original language.

- Refactoring and Maintenance. Consider how future changes in business processes may affect the validity of the sentences you choose. Be prepared to refactor identifiers in case the underlying processes change.

Broadly speaking, the implementation of sentence-based identifiers is a powerful design strategy that supports not only the understanding and maintenance of information systems but also reinforces the correspondence between the data and the business operations they represent.

When designing these identifiers, it is vital to consider not only clarity and accuracy but also practical application in the context of the business it is serving. Sentence identifiers work best when they are intuitive, relevant, and reflect the day-to-day operations of the organization.

13 Semantics as Cognitive Architecture in the Age of Artificial Intelligence.

The intersection between Artificial Intelligence (AI) and Data Semantics ushers in a new epistemology of information, in which language is not just a means of communication but an essential substrate for artificial cognition. With the advancement of Natural Language Processing (NLP) and Explainable AI (XAI), it becomes possible to extract semantic knowledge from data on scales never imagined, promoting not only automation but also interpretation and contextual inference.

13.1 Ontologies for Machine Learning and Explainable AI.

The increasing complexity of machine learning models demands semantic structures that ensure data transparency, interpretability, and interoperability. This challenge gains relevance with the advent of Explainable AI (XAI), whose goal is to ensure that algorithmic decisions can be interpreted and audited by humans.

13.1.1 The Role of Ontologies in the Semantic Structuring of AI.

Ontologies offer a formalized model for knowledge representation, providing conceptual hierarchies, axioms, and semantic relationships that aid in structuring data for machine learning. According to Guarino, Oberle, and Staab (2009), ontologies allow the formalization of specific domains, ensuring that AI models interpret data within a standardized context.

The impact of ontologies on machine learning can be described in three dimensions:

1. Reduction of Semantic Ambiguity: Ontologies impose formal restrictions on the interpretation of data, avoiding inconsistencies and semantic noise.

2. Improved Model Explainability: Allows algorithms to justify their inferences based on documented semantic rules.

3. Facilitation of Learning Transfer: Ontologies structure knowledge in a reusable way, allowing models to be adapted to new contexts without the need to start training from scratch.

In practice, ontologies such as Gene Ontology (GO) in biomedicine and FOAF (Friend of a Friend) in the Semantic Web exemplify how the formalization of concepts can improve the accuracy and reliability of AI systems.

13.1.2 Explainable AI and the Need for Semantic Representation.

One of the biggest challenges of modern AI is its cognitive opacity, that is, the inability to clearly explain the criteria used in its decisions. The use of ontologies in XAI allows you to create semantic trails that justify algorithmic inference.

For example, in recommendation systems, semantic ontologies can explain why a user received a certain suggestion from a network of formal relationships between preferences, contexts, and behavioral patterns. This approach is already being incorporated into initiatives such as IBM Watson and Google Knowledge Graph, which seek to make their algorithms more interpretable and auditable.

13.1.3 Natural Language Processing and Semantic Knowledge Extraction.

The evolution of Natural Language Processing (NLP) has transformed the way machines understand and process human knowledge. Advances in deep neural networks, semantic embeddings, and transformation models, such as BERT (Bidirectional Encoder Representations from Transformers) and GPT (Generative Pre-trained Transformer), have elevated the ability of machines to interpret nuances of language.

13.2   NLP Architectures and Semantic Modeling.

NLP relies on formal frameworks to understand and generate language in a meaningful way. Semantic models such as WordNet, ConceptNet, and FrameNet are essential for providing machines with a structured repertoire of relationships between words, concepts, and meanings.

NLP knowledge extraction occurs in three main steps:

- Tokenization and morphosyntactic analysis: word identification and grammatical structure.

- Semantic disambiguation: use of semantic models to avoid misinterpretations of polysemic words.

- Inference and knowledge generation: application of semantic rules to generate new insights from large volumes of textual data.

3.2. Advanced Applications of NLP in Knowledge Extraction

The application of NLP for knowledge extraction is already revolutionizing several areas, such as:

- "Jurimetrics: automated analysis of legal texts to predict judicial decisions.

- "Automated medical diagnosis: interpretation of clinical records to aid diagnoses based on biomedical literature.

- "Monitoring of disinformation: identification of semantic patterns to detect fake news on social networks.

The great frontier of semantic extraction via NLP lies in the combination of structured ontologies with deep learning, ensuring that generative models, such as ChatGPT and PaLM, can operate within interpretable and auditable semantic boundaries.

13.3   Implementation of Semantic Agents in Data Systems.

Semantic agents represent the evolution of the integration between Artificial Intelligence, Semantic Web, and Data Governance, operating as autonomous entities that extract, process, and interact with information in real time.

Semantic agents act as intelligent intermediaries, using formalized knowledge to optimize the interaction between humans and machines.

Among its main functions, the following stand out:

- Automated data curation: identification, enrichment, and validation of information in large repositories.

- Meaning-based process automation: autonomous decision-making guided by semantic rules.

- Interoperability between systems: integration of heterogeneous data through semantic standards such as RDF and OWL.

Examples of Semantic Agents in Application:

- Google Assistant and Alexa: use of semantic graphs to understand user intentions.

- "Regulatory Compliance Systems: semantic agents applied to monitor compliance with GDPR and LGPD.

- "Intelligent Industrial Automation: agents that use ontologies to optimize production processes.

The implementation of semantic agents represents a transformative paradigm, where data governance becomes self-adaptive and dynamic, eliminating traditional barriers to informational management.

14 Use Cases and Best Practices in Different Domains: The Application of Semantics for Digital Transformation.

The rise of data as a strategic asset has brought to light critical challenges related to the quality, interoperability, and standardization of information. In industries such as healthcare, finance, government, and industry 4.0, the lack of semantic alignment directly impacts operational efficiency, decision-making, and regulatory compliance.

The application of data semantics in these domains is not restricted to the simple organization of information; It becomes a competitive and regulatory differential, ensuring interoperability, intelligent automation, and informational transparency.

14.1 Health: Semantic Interoperability in Electronic Medical Records.

The healthcare industry is one of the sectors that benefits the most from semantic standardization, given the need for secure and accurate exchange of clinical information between different institutions and systems. The use of interconnected electronic medical records improves the quality of diagnoses, avoids redundancies in exams, and optimizes hospital management.

Without standardized semantics, electronic medical records become incomprehensible between different systems, resulting in problems such as:

- Lack of interoperability: Hospital systems use divergent nomenclatures and formats, making it difficult to integrate records.

- Errors and redundancies: patients undergoing repeated examinations due to the inability of systems to consolidate pre-existing information.

- Regulatory challenges: compliance with regulations such as HIPAA (USA), GDPR (Europe) and LGPD (Brazil) requires traceability and semantic interoperability.

- To ensure interoperability, several international standards have been adopted:

- HL7 FHIR (Fast Healthcare Interoperability Resources): defines a semantic model for the exchange of clinical data between systems.

- SNOMED CT (Systematized Nomenclature of Medicine: clinical Terms): A global medical ontology that standardizes medical terminologies.

- LOINC (Logical Observation Identifiers Names and Codes): standard for coding laboratory tests.

14.2   Use Case: Digital Transformation in the NHS (UK).

The UK's National Health Service (NHS) has implemented a strategy based on FHIR and SNOMED CT to integrate electronic health record systems at the national level. As a result:

- It reduced the costs of duplicate exams by 25%.

- It increased patient safety by ensuring that allergies and previous diagnoses were shared between hospitals.

- It facilitated the adoption of AI for clinical diagnosis, with learning based on standardized medical records.

14.3   Finance: Semantic Standardization for Fraud Prevention and Compliance

The financial industry deals with large volumes of sensitive data, requiring traceability and semantic integrity to prevent fraud and ensure regulatory compliance.

Challenges of Financial Data Governance:

- Discrepancies in accounting records: institutions use their own nomenclatures and standards, making audits more complex.

- Difficulty in detecting fraud: Anti-fraud models rely on solid semantic foundations to correlate suspicious transactions.

- Fragmented regulatory compliance: Regulations such as Basel III, GDPR, and Sarbanes-Oxley require traceability of financial data.

- Semantic Standards for Financial Data:

- "XBRL (eXtensible Business Reporting Language): semantic standard for financial reporting, ensuring uniformity in accounting.

- FIBO (Financial Industry Business Ontology): financial ontology standardized by the EDM Council, allowing interoperability between banks and regulators.

"ISO 20022: Global standard for semantic communication between banking institutions.

14.4   Use Case: Open Banking and Payment Interoperability.

Open Banking in the UK and EU uses ISO 20022-based semantic APIs, allowing customers to share their banking details securely. As benefits, the following stand out:

- Reduction of the risk of financial fraud, with semantic validation of transactions.

- Increased transparency in the granting of credit.

- Increased competition and innovation, allowing fintechs to access banking data in a standardized way.

14.5 Government and the Public Sector: Open Data and Semantic Transparency.

Transparency in public administration is a fundamental pillar of democratic governance. The use of semantic open data allows citizens, companies, and researchers to access and analyze public information in a structured way.

Problems in Government Data Management:

- Lack of standardization in data publication: agencies use heterogeneous formats (PDFs, spreadsheets without metadata).

- Difficulty of access and interoperability: Public data often lacks structured APIs.

- Lack of traceability: changes to public databases do not have clear versioning.

- Standards for Government Open Data:

- DCAT (Data Catalog Vocabulary): vocabulary to describe government datasets.

- schema.org for public data: Structures semantic metadata for easy indexing and querying.

- RDF and Linked Data: Enable the interconnection of global public data.

14.6 Use Case: European Union Open Data Portal.

The European Union has implemented a standardised open data portal in DCAT, resulting in:

- Ease of integrating data from different countries.

- Increased administrative transparency.

- Greater reuse of public data for innovation and research.

14.7 Industry 4.0: IoT and Semantic Data for Automation.

In Industry 4.0, semantic interoperability enables machines, sensors, and production systems to operate in a coordinated manner, reducing failures and optimizing processes.

Semantics Challenges in Industrial IoT:

- Difficulty in integrating heterogeneous sensors: equipment from different manufacturers uses different standards.

- Inconsistency in the interpretation of industrial events: lack of standardized semantic models hinders predictive analysis.

- Safety and reliability: Industrial environments demand semantic traceability to avoid critical failures.

Semantic Standards for IoT in Industry 4.0:

- W3C Web of Things (WoT): Standardizes ontologies for IoT devices.

- OPC-UA (Open Platform Communications Unified Architecture): defines a semantic model for data exchange in industrial automation.

- ISO/IEC 21838 Industrial Ontologies: formal framework for semantics in manufacturing.

14.8   Use Case: Smart Factories in Germany.

The Industrie 4.0 initiative in Germany uses OPC-UA and RDF to integrate machines and reduce operational failures. Benefits include:

- 20% reduction in machine downtime.
- Optimization of production processes via semantic machine learning.

15 Semantic Trends and Perspectives in the Age of Massive Data: Data Intelligence in Web 3.0 and Beyond.

The explosion in the volume of data in contemporary society, driven by the advancement of Artificial Intelligence (AI), the Internet of Things (IoT) and the Semantic Web, has radically reconfigured the way we interact with information. It's never been more crucial to ensure that data is not only stored but interpreted correctly, coherently organized, and intelligently accessible.

The transition to a new digital paradigm – characterized by Web 3.0, automation in semantic standardization, and the evolution of data dictionaries – suggests a scenario in which semantic governance will be an essential pillar for data intelligence.

15.1 Semantic Web and Web 3.0: The Impact on Data Management.

The Semantic Web, a concept initially proposed by Tim Berners-Lee (2001), established the basis for an internet in which data not only circulates but is interpretable by machines, ensuring interoperability and contextual intelligence. With the advancement of Web 3.0, this model evolves into a scenario in which decentralization and automation of data management become a reality.

15.1.1 The Semantic Web: From Syntax to Data Understanding.

In the Semantic Web, data is structured in a way that can be understood by intelligent systems.

For this, standards such as:

- RDF (Resource Description Framework): framework for semantic modeling of data.

- OWL (Web Ontology Language): formalization of ontologies to ensure logical inference.

- SPARQL (SPARQL Protocol and RDF Query Language): Semantic query language for structured data retrieval.

These technologies enable data to be interpreted contextually, eliminating ambiguities and promoting integration between heterogeneous sources of information.

15.1.2 Web 3.0 and the Paradigm of Semantic Decentralization.

Web 3.0 represents an evolution of the Semantic Web, introducing concepts such as blockchain, decentralized data (IPFS), and distributed intelligence. Its impacts on semantic data management include:

- Data Sovereignty and Autonomy: with the decentralization provided by blockchain technologies, users now have control over their own data, reducing dependence on large corporations.

- Full Interoperability: With the use of Linked Data and decentralized semantic networks, data can be shared between different platforms without loss of meaning.

- Smart Contracts and Semantic Data: the use of Smart Contracts allows semantic rules to be incorporated directly into digital transactions, ensuring compliance and automatic traceability.

These trends show that data semantics is not just a technical tool but a strategic element for the evolution of digital governance.

15.2   Automation and AI in Semantic Standardization.

The increasing complexity of data ecosystems requires automated solutions for semantic standardization. The integration between Artificial Intelligence and Semantic Governance becomes essential to ensure data quality, coherence, and interoperability.

15.2.1 AI and Machine Learning in Data Normalization.

The application of machine learning (ML) in semantic standardization has already demonstrated significant advances. AI models are used to:

- Detection of semantic inconsistencies: automatic identification of errors in heterogeneous databases.

- Ontology alignment: mapping of different semantic models to ensure compatibility.

- Automatic knowledge extraction: use of Natural Language Processing (NLP) to structure and enrich knowledge bases.

The use of semantic transformers, such as BERT and GPT, allows algorithms to understand complex patterns of relationship between data, optimizing semantic interoperability.

15.2.2 Knowledge Graphs and Data Fabric.

The evolution of semantic automation also involves the adoption of knowledge graphs and Data Fabric – data integration architectures based on semantic intelligence.

- Knowledge Graphs: structure information in an interconnected semantic network, allowing inference and reasoning about the data.

- Data Fabric: automates the standardization, integration, and governance of data using machine learning and computational semantics.

These approaches represent a paradigm shift in the way data is organized and accessed, reducing manual effort in semantic governance.

15.3   The Future of Data Dictionaries and Semantic Governance.

The evolution of semantic technologies also impacts data dictionaries and metadata, making them more dynamic and intelligent.

The data dictionaries of the future will be active systems, which:

- Continuous learning: they update definitions and classifications based on the use of data.

- Automatically detect anomalies: they use AI to identify semantic inconsistencies.

- Engage with users: Provide predictive insights into data quality and governance.

The concept of Active Metadata Management has already been applied on platforms such as Collibra and Alation, allowing for more flexible and responsive governance.

Another trend is the complete automation of semantic governance, where data rules and policies are managed as source code.

This allows you to:

- Automatic audits and compliance: Security and compliance policies are applied programmatically.

- Semantic versioning: Changes to data dictionaries are tracked and managed as code.

- Data workflow automation: Curation and standardization processes are executed without manual intervention.

This approach represents a breakthrough in the scalability of semantic governance, allowing large volumes of data to be managed with greater precision and efficiency.

15.4   The Future of Semantics in the Data Society.

The convergence between Semantic Web, AI, and Automation suggests a scenario where data is no longer static elements and becomes dynamic, intelligent, and self-adaptive entities. Semantic management of data will no longer be an isolated technical challenge but a central strategic factor for innovation, governance, and informational transparency.

Those who can master the complexity of semantics in the age of massive, distributed data will not only be optimizing processes but building the foundation for a new model of interconnected digital intelligence.

16 Test your knowledge.

16.1 Questions.

1. What is the main epistemological and technical challenge highlighted in the context of data governance in the information age?

a) The increasing speed of data generation.

(b) the need for more efficient storage infrastructure.

c) The requirement of a rigorous semantic architecture to ensure the intelligibility, interoperability and reliability of information.

d) Compliance with data privacy regulations.

2. According to Floridi (2011), what compromises the reliability of information in the global informational ecosystem?

a) The excess of technical standardization.

b) The lack of investment in data analysis technologies.

c) The absence of robust semantic criteria, generating the "infossmog".

d) The complexity of artificial intelligence algorithms.

3. What is the role of data ontologies in information governance, according to Guarino, Oberle and Staab (2009)?

a) Optimize the speed of data processing.

b) Ensure data security against cyber attacks.

c) To constitute formal representations of knowledge, establishing semantic relations between entities, attributes and concepts.

d) Facilitate the visualization of data in interactive dashboards.

4. What would Peirce (1955) describe as the result of the absence of well-defined ontologies and semantic rules in the derivation of meanings?

a) An increase in operational efficiency.

(b) An improvement in technical compliance.

c) An inconsistent interpretative abduction, leading to erroneous interpretations and structural contradictions in the data.

d) A simplification in data modeling.

5. What is the main focus of semantic governance, as discussed by Yu and He (2016)?

a) The physical integrity of the data servers.

(b) the security of data communication networks.

c) The rigorous management of the meanings attributed to data within an organization.

d) The optimization of data storage costs.

6. What are the three essential principles that underpin semantic standardization to ensure interoperability between different domains and applications?

a) Security, integrity and availability of data.

b) Speed, volume and variety of data.

c) Reuse of controlled vocabularies, formalization of semantic metadata and adoption of persistent identifiers.

d) Validation, verification and visualization of data.

7. How do models such as BERT (Devlin et al., 2018) contribute to the analysis of unstructured information?

a) Speeding up the transfer of data between different systems.

b) Increasing cloud data storage capacity.

c) Understanding the semantic context of the data, expanding the capacity for categorization and analysis.

d) Improving data security through advanced encryption.

8. What is the question that knowledge seeks to answer, in contrast to the question answered by information ("what happened?")?

a) "Where did it happen?"

b) "When did it happen?"

c) "Why did it happen?" and "What can happen next?".

d) "Who was involved?"

9. According to Polanyi (1966), what is a fundamental characteristic of human knowledge that hinders its integral transfer to formal systems?

a) Its static and immutable nature.

b) Its inherent complexity that requires large volumes of data.

c) To know more than we can express, emphasizing that a large part of human knowledge is tacit.

d) Its dependence on advanced visualization technologies.

10. What is the great challenge of modern organizations, as highlighted by Davenport and Prusak (1998), in relation to data?

a) Ensure data security against external threats.

b) Reduce data storage costs.

c) The ability to convert data into competitive advantage.

d) Increase the speed of data processing.

11. What is the purpose of the Semantic Web, according to Berners-Lee, Hendler and Lassila (2001)?

a) Increase the speed of internet browsing.

b) Create more intuitive user interfaces.

c) Build an infrastructure in which machines and humans can process and interpret data in an interoperable and contextualized way.

d) Reduce the energy consumption of web servers.

12. What are the three main levels at which the ontological approach to semantic interoperability can be organized?

a) Syntax, hardware and software.

b) Data, information and knowledge.

c) Security, integrity and availability.

d) Syntactic interoperability, semantic interoperability and ontologies.

13. In the health area, what ontology is used to standardize medical terminology in different hospital systems and electronic medical records?

a) Dublin Core.

b) RDF (Resource Description Framework).

c) OWL (Web Ontology Language).

d) SNOMED CT (Systematized Nomenclature of Medicine – Clinical Terms).

14. What does the use of DCAT (Data Catalog Vocabulary) enable in governments that implement semantic standards for public data?

a) Increase the security of government data.

b) Reduce data storage costs.

c) Integrate open data portals globally.

d) Improve the speed of access to data.

15. What is the representation of data in conceptual modeling?

a) Detailed, with specific tables and columns.

b) Physical, with a focus on performance and storage.

c) Abstract, focusing on the identification of the main entities and their relationships.

d) Logical, with normalizations and integrity restrictions.

16. What are the three main categories that metadata is classified into?

a) Data, information and knowledge.

b) Security, integrity and availability.

c) Descriptive metadata, structural metadata and administrative metadata.

d) Hardware, software and networks.

17. What is the importance of building a shared vocabulary through ontologies and taxonomies?

a) Increase the speed of data processing.

b) Reduce data storage costs.

c) Ensure semantic consistency, interoperability and efficient data governance.

d) Improve data security against external threats.

18. What is the main difference between taxonomies and ontologies in the structuring of controlled vocabularies?

a) Taxonomies are more complex and require greater technical knowledge.

b) Ontologies are simpler and easier to implement.

c) Taxonomies structure concepts in hierarchical classifications, while ontologies formalize relations and semantic rules.

d) Taxonomies are used only in libraries, while ontologies are used in corporate systems.

19. What are the fundamental elements of an ontology?

a) Data, information and knowledge.

b) Hardware, software and networks.

c) Security, integrity and availability.

d) Concepts, relations, axioms and instances.

20. What are some good practices for building an effective shared vocabulary?

a) Use only technical terms and avoid the participation of business users.

b) Prioritize the complexity and sophistication of semantic models.

c) Adopt recognized standards, use modeling tools, create an institutional glossary, and promote semantic governance.

d) Ignoring the need for periodic updating and revision of vocabularies.

21. What is the role of metadata in the growing digitization of production processes and in the increase in the volume of data?

a) Optimize the performance of hardware systems.

b) Reduce cloud data storage costs.

c) Provide structured descriptions of the data, allowing disparate systems to exchange information in a consistent manner.

d) Ensure data security against cyber attacks.

22. What are the principles known as FAIR Data Principles, which are promoted by metadata standards?

(a) Flexibility, adaptability, interoperability and accountability.

b) Ease, accessibility, intelligibility and relevance.

c) Findability, accessibility, interoperability and reuse.

d) Format, storage, integrity and retrieval.

23. What are the key metadata standards adopted globally?

a) XML, JSON, CSV and HTML.

b) TCP/IP, HTTP, FTP and SMTP.

c) Dublin Core (DCMI), Resource Description Framework (RDF), Web Ontology Language (OWL) and Simple Knowledge Organization System (SKOS).

d) SQL, NoSQL, MySQL and PostgreSQL.

24. What are the fundamental elements defined by the Dublin Core standard for the description of a resource?

a) Hardware, software, networks and users.

b) Security, integrity, availability and authenticity.

c) Title, creator, subject, description, publisher, date and type.

d) Format, size, location and version.

25. How do semantic standardization and normalization contribute to data quality?

a) Increasing the speed of data processing.

b) Reducing data storage costs.

c) Ensuring that data is interpretable, reusable, and integrable in an efficient manner.

d) Improving data security against unauthorized access.

26. What are the elements that are usually included in data dictionaries?

a) Hardware, software, networks and users.

b) Security, integrity, availability and authenticity.

c) Field name, description, type of data, constraints and relationships.

d) Format, size, location and version.

27. What are metadata catalogs and what is their main function?

a) They are repositories of raw data for later analysis.

b) They are tools for data visualization in real time.

c) They are centralized repositories that organize and document metadata from different data sources, allowing the indexing, crawling, and discovery of information in various systems.

d) They are security systems to protect data against unauthorized access.

28. What is the definition of a semantic component in the context of information systems and databases?

a) A hardware unit responsible for data processing.

b) A complex algorithm used for data analysis.

c) A basic unit of meaning within a language or system, which contributes to the understanding or interpretation of a more complex expression.

d) A security protocol to protect the integrity of the data.

29. What is the role of a short form in the communication and representation of information in data systems?

a) Increase the complexity and sophistication of the language used.

b) Prioritize the aesthetics and visual presentation of the data.

c) Act as a condensed version of one or more words, maintaining communication efficiency while saving space and effort.

d) Reduce the importance of documentation and data glossary.

30. What are the two types of short forms mentioned in the text?

a) Simple and compound short forms.

b) Explicit and implicit short-forms.

c) Technical and non-technical short-forms.

d) Natural and derived short-forms.

31. How is identification used in information systems and data modeling?

a) To restrict access to data to authorized users only.

b) To optimize the speed of data processing.

c) To create unique and meaningful identifiers for data elements, distinguishing them and clearly conveying their meaning and context.

d) To ensure data security against cyberattacks.

32. What is the importance of using consistent nomenclatures in the development of information systems?

a) Increasing the complexity of the code to make reverse engineering difficult.

b) Reduce the need for documentation and comments in the code.

c) Facilitate understanding, teamwork, maintenance and development of more organized software.

d) Prioritize the aesthetics and visual presentation of the code.

33. How important is it to be descriptive but concise when naming identifiers in a data system?

a) Reduce code compilation time.

b) Decrease the size of data files.

c) Communicate the function or content of a variable or field clearly, without forcing the user to decipher an excessively long or complex name.

d) Increasing the complexity of the code to make reverse engineering difficult.

34. What is the recommendation on the use of obscure abbreviations in the naming of identifiers?

a) Use obscure abbreviations to save space and typing time.

b) Prioritize abbreviations that are known exclusively to the development team.

c) Avoid the use of obscure abbreviations to avoid confusion and ensure clear communication.

d) Document all obscure abbreviations in a separate glossary.

35. How can the use of prefixes and suffixes contribute to clarity and organization in the nomenclature of data and structures?

a) Making names more complex and difficult to understand.

b) Reducing the need for documentation and comments in the code.

c) Indicating the type of data (prefixes) and the structure or purpose of an element (suffixes), facilitating the understanding of the code.

d) Standardizing the use of obscure abbreviations to save space.

36. Why is it important to maintain proper specificity in identifying data or systems?

a) To hinder identification and access to data by unauthorized users.

b) To reduce the amount of metadata and documentation required.

c) To avoid confusion, identifying each element in a specific way and indicating its function or purpose.

d) To optimize the speed of data processing and storage.

37. What is the recommendation on the use of numbers in identifiers?

a) Use sequential numbers to facilitate the organization and ordering of data.

b) Prioritize numbers that are significant in specific contexts.

c) Avoid the use of numbers in identifiers, as this practice can lead to confusion and difficulties in understanding and maintaining the system in the long term.

d) Document all numbers used in identifiers in a separate glossary.

38. What is the importance of adopting word-forming standards in systems and projects?

a) Increasing the complexity of the code to make reverse engineering difficult.

b) Reduce the need for documentation and comments in the code.

c) Maintain consistency and organization, facilitating understanding and collaboration between developers from different countries.

d) Prioritize the aesthetics and visual presentation of the code.

39. What is the importance of documentation in technological projects, especially in relation to the data dictionary?

a) Reduce the development and implementation time of the project.

b) Reduce the need for testing and validation of the code.

c) Ensure that all team members can understand what was done, how it was done, and why certain design decisions were made.

d) Prioritize the aesthetics and visual presentation of the project.

40. Why is it important to be aware of business conventions when creating nomenclatures in information systems?

a) To hinder access to data by unauthorized users.

b) To reduce the need for training and support to users.

c) To facilitate understanding and collaboration between technical staff and business users, strengthening the cohesion and overall strategy of the company.

d) To optimize the speed of data processing and storage.

41. How important is it to plan identifiers with scalability in mind?

a) Reduce the initial cost of developing the system.

b) Reduce the need for testing and validation of the code.

c) Ensure that identifiers behave well with system expansions, preventing them from becoming obsolete or inadequate as the system grows and evolves.

d) Prioritize the aesthetics and visual presentation of the system.

42. What is the importance of reusing established identifiers in systems development?

a) Reduce code size and optimize system performance.

b) Reduce the need for documentation and comments in the code.

c) Create a sense of familiarity and continuity, promote a smoother learning curve, facilitate code maintenance, and avoid unnecessary increase in complexity.

d) Prioritize the aesthetics and visual presentation of the system.

43. How does referencing promote consistency and understanding across systems and databases?

a) Restricting access to data to authorized users only.

b) Optimizing the speed of data processing.

c) Reusing already established nomenclatures for data elements with well-understood semantics, maintaining semantic integrity and facilitating the interpretation of the data.

d) Ensuring data security against cyberattacks.

44. What is the role of qualification in the nomenclature of information systems?

a) Reduce the amount of metadata and documentation required.

b) Restrict access to data to authorized users only.

c) Add specificity and clarity to an identifier to ensure that it conveys its purpose and context unambiguously.

d) Optimize the speed of data processing and storage.

45. How do sentence-based identifiers contribute to clarity and comprehension in data systems?

a) Restricting access to data to authorized users only.

b) Optimizing the speed of data processing.

c) Capturing and transmitting an action or functionality represented by a given data or process, clarifying not only the nature of a data entity but also the active role it plays.

d) Ensuring data security against cyberattacks.

46. What is the role of ontologies in the semantic structuring of AI?

a) Increase the complexity of machine learning algorithms.

b) Reduce the need for data for training AI models.

c) Offer a formalized model for knowledge representation, assisting in the structuring of data for machine learning and ensuring that AI models interpret data within a standardized context.

d) Optimize the processing speed of the data used by AI.

47. How does Natural Language Processing (NLP) contribute to the extraction of semantic knowledge?

a) Increasing the complexity of data analysis algorithms.

b) Reducing the need for data for semantic analysis.

c) Transforming the way machines understand and process human knowledge, increasing the ability of machines to interpret nuances of language.

d) Optimizing the processing speed of textual data.

48. How does the healthcare industry benefit from semantic interoperability in electronic health records?

a) Reducing the need for clinical examinations.

b) Optimizing the speed of access to patient data.

c) Improving the quality of diagnoses, avoiding redundancies in exams and optimizing hospital management.

d) Increasing the security of patient data against unauthorized access.

49. How do the Semantic Web and Web 3.0 impact data management?

a) Increasing the centralization of data control.

b) Reducing the need for data standardization.

c) Laying the foundation for an internet in which data not only circulates but is interpretable by machines, ensuring interoperability and contextual intelligence, evolving into a scenario in which decentralization and automation of data management become a reality.

d) Prioritizing the aesthetics and visual presentation of data on the web.

50. What are the main challenges and opportunities for the practical implementation of data semantics?

a) Reduction of the complexity of information systems and optimization of data processing speed.

b) Reduction of the need for data standardization and increased security against cyber attacks.

c) Data heterogeneity and fragmentation, lack of skills and knowledge, resistance to change, implementation costs and technical complexity, balanced with improved decision-making, interoperability optimization, compliance and automatic auditing, automation and cost reduction, and personalization and contextual intelligence.

d) Prioritization of aesthetics and visual presentation of data and reduction of the need for documentation.

16.2 Answers.

1. c) The requirement of a rigorous semantic architecture to ensure the intelligibility, interoperability and reliability of information.

2. c) The absence of robust semantic criteria, generating the "infossmog".

3. c) To constitute formal representations of knowledge, establishing semantic relations between entities, attributes and concepts.

4. c) An inconsistent interpretive abduction, leading to erroneous interpretations and structural contradictions in the data.

5. c) The rigorous management of the meanings attributed to data within an organization.

6. c) Reuse of controlled vocabularies, formalization of semantic metadata and adoption of persistent identifiers.

7. c) Understanding the semantic context of the data, expanding the capacity for categorization and analysis.

8. c) "Why did it happen?" and "What can happen next?".

9. c) To know more than we can express, emphasizing that much of human knowledge is tacit.

10. c) The ability to convert data into competitive advantage.

11. c) Build an infrastructure in which machines and humans can process and interpret data in an interoperable and contextualized way.

12. d) Syntactic interoperability, semantic interoperability and ontologies

13. d) SNOMED CT (Systematized Nomenclature of Medicine – Clinical Terms)

14. c) Integrating open data portals globally

15. c) Abstract, focusing on the identification of the main entities and their relationships

16. c) Descriptive metadata, structural metadata and administrative metadata

17. c) Ensure semantic consistency, interoperability and efficient data governance

18. c) Taxonomies structure concepts in hierarchical classifications, while ontologies formalize relations and semantic rules

19. d) Concepts, relations, axioms and instances

20. c) Adopt recognized standards, use modeling tools, create an institutional glossary, and promote semantic governance

21. c) Provide structured descriptions of the data, allowing disparate systems to exchange information in a consistent manner

22. c) Findability, accessibility, interoperability and reuse

23. c) Dublin Core (DCMI), Resource Description Framework (RDF), Web Ontology Language (OWL) and Simple Knowledge Organization System (SKOS)

24. c) Title, creator, subject, description, publisher, date and type

25. c) Ensuring that data is interpretable, reusable, and integrable in an efficient manner

26. c) Field name, description, data type, constraints, and relationships

27. c) They are centralized repositories that organize and document metadata from different data sources, allowing the indexing, crawling, and discovery of information in various systems

28. c) A basic unit of meaning within a language or system, which contributes to the understanding or interpretation of a more complex expression

29. c) Act as a condensed version of one or more words, maintaining communication efficiency while saving space and effort

30. d) Natural and derived short-forms

31. c) To create unique and meaningful identifiers for data elements, distinguishing them and clearly conveying their meaning and context

32. c) Facilitate understanding, teamwork, maintenance and development of more organized software

33. c) Communicate the function or content of a variable or field clearly, without forcing the user to decipher an excessively long or complex name

34. c) Avoid the use of obscure abbreviations to avoid confusion and ensure clear communication

35. c) Indicating the type of data (prefixes) and the structure or purpose of an element (suffixes), facilitating the understanding of the code

36. c) To avoid confusion, identifying each element in a specific way and indicating its function or purpose

37. c) Avoid the use of numbers in identifiers, as this practice can lead to confusion and difficulties in understanding and maintaining the system in the long term

38. c) Maintain consistency and organization, facilitating understanding and collaboration between developers from different countries

39. c) Ensure that all team members can understand what was done, how it was done, and why certain design decisions were made

40. c) To facilitate understanding and collaboration between technical staff and business users, strengthening the cohesion and overall strategy of the company

41. c) Ensure that identifiers behave well with system expansions, preventing them from becoming obsolete or inadequate as the system grows and evolves

42. c) Create a sense of familiarity and continuity, promote a smoother learning curve, facilitate code maintenance, and avoid unnecessary increase in complexity

43. c) Reusing already established nomenclatures for data elements with well-understood semantics, maintaining semantic integrity and facilitating the interpretation of data

44. c) Add specificity and clarity to an identifier to ensure that it conveys its purpose and context unambiguously

45. c) Capturing and transmitting an action or functionality represented by a given data or process, clarifying not only the nature of a data entity but also the active role it plays

46. c) Offer a formalized model for knowledge representation, assisting in the structuring of data for machine learning and ensuring that AI models interpret data within a standardized context

47. c) Transforming the way machines understand and process human knowledge by enhancing the ability of machines to interpret nuances of language

48. c) Improving the quality of diagnoses, avoiding redundancies in exams and optimizing hospital management

49. c) Laying the foundation for an internet in which data not only circulates but is interpretable by machines, ensuring interoperability and contextual intelligence, evolving into a scenario in which decentralization and automation of data management become a reality

50. c) Data heterogeneity and fragmentation, lack of skills and knowledge, resistance to change, implementation costs, and technical complexity, balanced with improved decision-making, interoperability optimization, compliance and automatic auditing, automation and cost reduction, and personalization and contextual intelligence

17 Final Thoughts.

Throughout this book, we have explored information semantics as one of the fundamental pillars for data governance and artificial intelligence. We look at how standardization and semantic structuring are essential to ensure data quality, interoperability, and intelligibility in complex environments.

We address the difference between data, information, and knowledge, demonstrating how the hierarchy of knowledge influences data-driven decision-making.

We also understand the impact of semantics on data modeling, metadata management, and the construction of shared vocabularies, discussing patterns such as RDF, OWL, SKOS, and Linked Data. We analyze how these technologies underpin the Semantic Web and enable intelligent automation of processes in various sectors, such as healthcare, finance, government, and industry 4.0. Finally, we reflect on the future of semantic standardization in the era of Web 3.0 and artificial intelligence.

This book is just one of the pillars for a deeper understanding of data intelligence. If you want to master all the fundamental aspects of data governance and AI, I invite you to continue your journey with the other books in the Data Governance collection. Each volume taps into a critical component of this ecosystem, allowing you to build a solid foundation for acting strategically in the world of data.

The digital age requires professionals prepared to interpret, structure, and govern information accurately. If you want to be one step ahead in digital transformation, the next book in this collection will be your best choice. Continue reading, deepen your knowledge and transform your relationship with data.

18 Bibliography.

ACKOFF, R. L. (1989). From Data to Wisdom. Journal of Applied Systems Analysis, v. 16, p. 3-9.

ANGLES, R.; GUTIÉRREZ, C. (2008). Survey of Graph Database Models. ACM Computing Surveys, v. 40, n. 1, p. 1-39.

BERNERS-LEE, T. (2006). Linked Data: Design Issues. W3C.

BERNERS-LEE, T.; HENDLER, J.; LASSILA, O. (2001). The Semantic Web. Scientific American, v. 284, n. 5, p. 34-43.

CHEN, P. P. (1976). The Entity-Relationship Model: Toward a Unified View of Data. ACM Transactions on Database Systems, v. 1, n. 1, p. 9-36.

CODD, E. F. (1970). A Relational Model of Data for Large Shared Data Banks. Communications of the ACM, v. 13, n. 6, p. 377-387.

DAVENPORT, T. H.; PRUSAK, L. (1998). Working Knowledge: How Organizations Manage What They Know. Harvard Business Review Press.

DEVLIN, J.; CHANG, M.; LEE, K.; TOUTANOVA, K. (2018). BERT: Pre-training of Deep Bidirectional Transformers for Language Understanding. arXiv preprint arXiv:1810.04805.

EDM Council. (2020). FIBO Ontology: A Reference Standard for Financial Data.

EUZENAT, J.; SHVAIKO, P. (2013). Ontology Matching. Springer.

FLORIDI, L. (2011). The Philosophy of Information. Oxford University Press.

GRUBER, T. R. (1993). A Translation Approach to Portable Ontology Specifications. Knowledge Acquisition, v. 5, n. 2, p. 199-220.

GUARINO, N.; OBERLE, D.; STAAB, S. (2009). What is an Ontology?. In: Staab, S.; Studer, R. (Eds.). Handbook on Ontologies. Springer, p. 1-17.

HEATH, T.; BIZER, C. (2011). Linked Data: Evolving the Web into a Global Data Space. Morgan & Claypool.

ISO 20022. (2021). Financial Services – Universal Financial Industry Message Scheme.

MITCHELL, M. (2019). Artificial Intelligence: A Guide for Thinking Humans. Farrar, Straus and Giroux.

NONAKA, I.; TAKEUCHI, H. (1995). The Knowledge-Creating Company: How Japanese Companies Create the Dynamics of Innovation. Oxford University Press.

POLANYI, M. (1966). The Tacit Dimension. University of Chicago Press.

SINGH, H.; RAJAN, M. (2021). Metadata Management in Data Lakes: Principles, Techniques, and Tools. Springer.

STONEBRAKER, M. (2010). SQL Databases vs. NoSQL Databases. Communications of the ACM, v. 53, n. 4, p. 10-11.

W3C. (2017). Web of Things (WoT) Architecture.

WILKINSON, M. D. et al. (2016). The FAIR Guiding Principles for scientific data management and stewardship. Scientific Data, v. 3, n. 1, p. 160018.

YU, H.; HE, Y. (2016). Semantic Governance: Managing Data with Meaning. Journal of Information Science, v. 42, n. 2, p. 174-191.

19 Discover the Data Governance collection: The Knowledge That Highlights Companies and Professionals in the Information Age.

Information is now the most valuable asset. As a consequence, data governance is no longer a differentiator — it is a non-negotiable necessity. The Data Governance collection, for sale on Amazon, offers a complete, technical, and strategic approach for those who want to understand, structure, and apply the principles of data governance in the corporate and academic landscape.

Whether you're a manager, data scientist, information analyst, or strategic decision maker, this collection is indispensable for mastering data quality, security, semantics, and standardization.

19.1 What Will You Find in the Collection?

Each volume of the "Data Governance" collection explores an essential aspect of this universe, bringing fundamental concepts, practical applications, and critical reflections on the relationship between information, technology, and society.

Invest in Your Knowledge and Stand Out in the Information Age!

- The Data Governance Collection is more than a set of books — it is a passport to information mastery in an increasingly data-driven world.

- Learn from a recognized expert in the field of data intelligence, semantics, and corporate governance: Prof. Marcão.

- Get access to high-quality content, based on the most current and applicable standards in the market.

- Transform your view on data governance and structuring, gaining a competitive advantage in your career.

GET YOUR COMPLETE COLLECTION ON AMAZON NOW!

19.2   Why Is This Collection Essential for You?

Deepen your knowledge!

> More than books, this collection offers a structured learning journey, guiding the reader from the theoretical foundation to the practical application of data governance.

Practical and Direct Application!

> Companies that adopt good data governance practices have 40% less risk of inconsistency in decision-making processes and increase the efficiency of their data operations by 30%. This collection teaches you how to apply governance in corporate reality.

Position Yourself Ahead of the Market!

> The data-driven culture is one of the pillars of digital transformation. Professionals who master information management are increasingly valued in sectors such as banking, healthcare, technology, and public services.

Connect Data and Strategy!

> The world's most innovative organizations – Amazon, Google, Microsoft, and IBM – base their operations on structured data, intelligent semantics, and robust governance. With this collection, you'll learn how these companies turn data into competitive advantage.

Adapt to the Future of Information!

> With the rise of Artificial Intelligence and Web 3.0, semantic standardization and data governance have become fundamental to the interoperability and reliability of

19.3   Get to know the books in the Collection.

19.3.1 FUNDAMENTALS OF DATA GOVERNANCE.

Discover the hidden power of effective data governance! This book reveals the secrets that separate elite organizations from middling ones, offering a complete overview of modeling, quality, and essential frameworks such as DAMA-DMBOK and ISO 8000.

In a world where bad data costs millions, you can't ignore the fundamentals laid out here. Learn how to structure information that ensures accurate and reliable decisions.

The digital revolution requires professionals who master these techniques. Be the one leading this transformation or be left behind. Invest now in the knowledge that will be your competitive advantage and open doors to opportunities that others do not even see.

19.3.2 INFORMATION - INFORMATION SCIENCE - TECHNOLOGY - PROFESSION: CONCEPTS EXPLAINED.

WARNING: As you read this, 87% of careers are being quietly redefined by the information revolution! This essential guide reveals the concepts that separate leaders from followers in the new economy.

Uncover the true nature of the information that large organizations already exploit as a competitive advantage. Understand why Information Science has become the invisible differential of the most requested professionals.

The most valued skills on the market are here! Mastering these concepts is not optional – it is the difference between thriving or disappearing professionally.

Visionaries have already realized: those who understand these fundamentals today will control the most valuable resources of tomorrow. Invest now in knowledge that will open doors that others will not even know exist!

19.3.3 EASY-TO-UNDERSTAND INFORMATION - GLOSSARY AND FREQUENTLY ASKED QUESTIONS.

The secret dictionary that data experts don't want you to know! Instantly uncover technical terms that block your career advancement and prevent you from participating in strategic discussions.

While others spend hours researching concepts like "data lineage" and "semantic modeling," you'll have immediate answers and practical examples at your fingertips. This guide turns confusion into clarity in seconds!

Imagine impressing colleagues and superiors with your mastery of AI and data governance. The opportunities that will arise when you confidently speak the language of the experts!

Don't waste any more time trying to decipher complex terms. Invest now in this essential shortcut for your professional evolution!

19.3.4 SEMANTICS AND POWER OF DATA: CONSISTENCY, GOVERNANCE AND STANDARDIZATION.

Why do some companies extract billions from their information while others sink into worthless data? This essential guide lays out how data semantics quietly determine winners and losers in the digital age.

Discover how RDF and OWL models turn chaotic data into strategic gold. While amateurs discuss data volume, visionary professionals master the semantic consistency that drives AI and accurate predictive analytics.

Web 3.0 is already here and only organizations with semantic governance will survive! Don't risk being left behind while your competitors achieve seamless interoperability between systems.

Invest now in the knowledge that separates digital leaders from obsolete followers!

19.3.5 INFORMATION ARCHITECTURE: STRUCTURING CORPORATE KNOWLEDGE.

FIND OUT why some companies extract billions from your information while others sink into worthless data! This definitive guide lays out how information architecture quietly determines market leaders.

Master taxonomies and ontologies that turn chaotic data into accurate decisions. While your competitors are still debating basic concepts, you'll implement advanced frameworks like Data Fabric and Data Mesh that have already been tested by elite organizations.

The most successful CDOs already know: structuring corporate knowledge isn't just a technical advantage – it's the difference between surviving or leading in the digital economy.

Invest now in the knowledge that transforms information into your most valuable asset!

19.3.6 HIDDEN ASSETS – THE CHALLENGE OF GOVERNANCE BEYOND DATABASES.

Your organization is leaving millions in value hidden in the data that no one sees! As long as you focus only on structured databases, the true competitive advantage remains invisible in three overlooked treasures: unstructured data, semi-structured data, and tacit knowledge of your team.

Visionary leaders have already figured it out: whoever maps and governs these hidden assets quietly dominates the market. This revolutionary guide reveals proven methods for turning emails, documents, and your employees' experience into superior strategic decisions.

The new economy belongs to those who see beyond the tables! Don't risk being left behind while your competitors exploit informational riches that you don't even realize you have.

Invest now in the knowledge that will turn invisible data into your most valuable asset!

19.3.7 THE HUMAN FACTOR IN DATA GOVERNANCE.

This groundbreaking book reveals how conscious people and decisions can transform your data strategy. Focusing on organizational culture, ethics, and change management, the book is mandatory reading for Chief Data Officers, managers, scientists, and analysts who want to go beyond technical frameworks.

Discover how governance maturity depends on a deep understanding of ethical challenges, accountability in democratizing data access, and leadership.

This book invites you to reflect and act: put the human being at the center of decisions and achieve solid and sustainable results.

19.3.8 ONTOLOGY COLLECTION FOR DATA GOVERNANCE.

In today's corporate universe, where data abounds but insights are scarce, the ontological understanding of information emerges as the differentiating competence between ordinary professionals and visionary leaders.

Prof. Marcão's "Ontology for Data Governance" collection reveals the paradigms that are revolutionizing how innovative organizations structure and leverage their knowledge assets. Each concise volume unfolds crucial elements of this field—from philosophical foundations to practical implementations—with immediate applicability.

For CDOs and architects, these books offer solutions to semantic interoperability challenges. For data scientists, they reveal how ontological structures power machine learning algorithms. For executives, they present the path to turning fragmented data into actionable knowledge.

Purchase the collection now and become the architect of the knowledge your organization needs.

The collection consists of the following books:

1 - FUNDAMENTALS OF ONTOLOGY FOR DATA GOVERNANCE.

It explores how semantic structuring and standardization of information enhance data quality, interoperability, and intelligence, making governance more efficient and strategic.

2 - PRACTICAL APPLICATIONS AND METHODOLOGIES FOR THE DEVELOPMENT OF ONTOLOGY.

It presents strategies and frameworks for effective semantic modeling, ensuring interoperability, standardization, and intelligence in data management and governance.

3 - CASE STUDIES IN ONTOLOGY ENGINEERING.

It addresses real-world implementations of ontologies, demonstrating how semantic modeling transforms data governance, interoperability, and organizational intelligence across different industries.

4 - ADVANCED TECHNICAL ASPECTS, TOOLS AND THE FUTURE OF ONTOLOGIES.

The work delves into emerging technologies, frameworks and cutting-edge methodologies for ontology development and management, highlighting trends that will shape data governance and artificial intelligence.

19.3.9 MONETIZATION   AND   INFORMATION-BASED   BUSINESS
        MODELS.

It is an indispensable guide to understanding how companies, platforms, and governments are profiting from the data economy. Aimed at executives, digital business experts, and researchers, it offers powerful strategies for monetizing information, highlighting ethical and regulatory challenges, artificial intelligence, blockchain, and essential technological infrastructure.

Learn from real cases of the world's largest companies and discover how to turn data into wealth, creating strong, secure and sustainable competitive advantages in the digital landscape.

19.3.10   DATA GOVERNANCE DEPLOYMENT GUIDE.

Essential guide for organizations that want to implement, in practice, structured and efficient data governance.

Aimed at managers, analysts, and IT professionals, the book provides a detailed step-by-step: quickly assess current maturity, clearly define roles and responsibilities by creating a Data Governance Office (DGO), implement effective access, privacy, and regulatory compliance policies, and learn how to monitor results with actionable metrics.

Convert theory into real results and make your company a reference in strategic data management.

20 Big Data Collection: Unlocking the Future of Data in an Essential Collection.

The "Big Data" collection was created to be an indispensable guide for professionals, students, and enthusiasts who want to confidently navigate the vast and fascinating universe of data. In an increasingly digital and interconnected world, Big Data is not just a tool, but a fundamental strategy for the transformation of businesses, processes, and decisions. This collection sets out to simplify complex concepts and empower your readers to turn data into valuable insights.

Each volume in the collection addresses an essential component of this area, combining theory and practice to offer a broad and integrated understanding. You'll find themes such as:

In addition to exploring the fundamentals, the collection also looks into the future, with discussions on emerging trends such as the integration of artificial intelligence, text analytics, and governance in increasingly dynamic and global environments.

Whether you are a manager looking for ways to optimize processes, a data scientist exploring new techniques, or a beginner curious to understand the impact of data on everyday life, the Big Data collection is the ideal partner on this journey. Each book has been developed with accessible yet technically sound language, allowing readers of all levels to advance their understanding and skills.

Get ready to master the power of data and stand out in an ever-evolving market. The Big Data collection is available on Amazon and is the key to unlocking the future of data-driven intelligence.

20.1   Why Is This Collection Essential for You?

The Big Data collection is designed to cater to a diverse audience that shares the goal of understanding and applying the power of data in an increasingly information-driven world. Whether you're a seasoned professional or just starting your journey in the technology and data space, this collection offers valuable insights, practical examples, and indispensable tools.

1. Technology and Data Professionals.

Data scientists, data engineers, analysts, and developers will find in the collection the fundamentals they need to master concepts such as Big Data Analytics, distributed computing, Hadoop, and advanced tools. Each volume covers technical topics in a practical way, with clear explanations and examples that can be applied in everyday life.

2. Managers and Organizational Leaders.

For leaders and managers, the collection offers a strategic view on how to implement and manage Big Data projects. The books show how to use data to optimize processes, identify opportunities, and make informed decisions. Real-world examples illustrate how companies have used Big Data to transform their businesses into industries such as retail, healthcare, and the environment.

3. Entrepreneurs and Small Businesses.

Entrepreneurs and small business owners who want to leverage the power of data to improve their competitiveness can also benefit. The collection presents practical strategies for using Big Data in a scalable way, demystifying the idea that this technology is exclusive to large corporations.

4. Students and Beginners in the Area.

If you're a student or just starting to explore the universe of Big Data, this collection is the perfect starting point. With accessible language and practical examples, the books make complex concepts more understandable, preparing you to dive deeper into data science and artificial intelligence.

5. Curious and Technology Enthusiasts.

For those who, even outside of the corporate or academic environment, have an interest in understanding how Big Data is shaping the world, the collection offers a fascinating and educational introduction. Discover how data is transforming areas as diverse as health, sustainability, and human behavior.

Regardless of your level of expertise or the industry in which you operate, the Big Data collection is designed to empower your readers with actionable insights, emerging trends, and a comprehensive view of the future of data. If you're looking to understand and apply the power of Big Data to grow professionally or transform your business, this collection is for you. Available on Amazon, it is the essential guide to mastering the impact of data in the digital age.

20.2   Get to know the books in the Collection.

20.2.1 SIMPLIFYING BIG DATA INTO 7 CHAPTERS.

This book is an essential guide for anyone who wants to understand and apply the fundamental concepts of Big Data in a clear and practical way. In a straightforward and accessible format, the book covers everything from theoretical pillars, such as the 5 Vs of Big Data, to modern tools and techniques, including Hadoop and Big Data Analytics.

Exploring real examples and strategies applicable in areas such as health, retail, and the environment, this work is ideal for technology professionals, managers, entrepreneurs, and students looking to transform data into valuable insights.

With an approach that connects theory and practice, this book is the perfect starting point for mastering the Big Data universe and leveraging its possibilities.

20.2.2 BIG DATA MANAGEMENT.

This book offers a practical and comprehensive approach to serving a diverse audience, from beginner analysts to experienced managers, students, and entrepreneurs.

With a focus on the efficient management of large volumes of information, this book presents in-depth analysis, real-world examples, comparisons between technologies such as Hadoop and Apache Spark, and practical strategies to avoid pitfalls and drive success.

Each chapter is structured to provide applicable insights, from the fundamentals to advanced analytics tools.

20.2.3 BIG DATA ARCHITECTURE.

This book is intended for a diverse audience, including data architects who need to build robust platforms, analysts who want to understand how data layers integrate, and executives who are looking to inform informed decisions. Students and researchers in computer science, data engineering, and management will also find here a solid and up-to-date reference.

The content combines a practical approach and conceptual rigor. You'll be guided from the fundamentals, such as the 5 Vs of Big Data, to the complexity of layered architectures, spanning infrastructure, security, analytics tools, and storage standards like Data Lake and Data Warehouse. In addition, clear examples, real case studies, and technology comparisons will help turn theoretical knowledge into practical applications and effective strategies.

20.2.4 BIG DATA IMPLEMENTATION.

This volume has been carefully crafted to be a practical and accessible guide, connecting theory to practice for professionals and students who want to master the strategic implementation of Big Data solutions.

It covers everything from quality analysis and data integration to topics such as real-time processing, virtualization, security, and governance, offering clear and applicable examples.

20.2.5 STRATEGIES TO REDUCE COSTS AND MAXIMIZE BIG DATA INVESTMENTS.

With a practical and reasoned approach, this book offers detailed analysis, real case studies and strategic solutions for IT managers, data analysts, entrepreneurs and business professionals.

This book is an indispensable guide to understanding and optimizing the costs associated with implementing Big Data, covering everything from storage and processing to small business-specific strategies and cloud cost analysis.

As part of the "Big Data" collection, it connects to other volumes that deeply explore the technical and strategic dimensions of the field, forming an essential library for anyone seeking to master the challenges and opportunities of the digital age.

20.2.6 700 Big Data Questions Collection.

This collection is designed to provide dynamic, challenging, and hands-on learning. With 700 questions strategically crafted and distributed in 5 volumes, it allows you to advance in the domain of Big Data in a progressive and engaging way. Each answer is an opportunity to expand your vision and apply concepts realistically and effectively.

The collection consists of the following books:

1   BIG DATA: 700 QUESTIONS - VOLUME 1.

It deals with information as the raw material for everything, the fundamental concepts and applications of Big Data.

2   BIG DATA: 700 QUESTIONS - VOLUME 2.

It addresses Big Data in the context of information science, data technology trends and analytics, Augmented analytics, continuous intelligence, distributed computing, and latency.

3   BIG DATA: 700 QUESTIONS - VOLUME 3.

It contemplates the technological and management aspects of Big Data, data mining, classification trees, logistic regression and professions in the context of Big Data.

4   BIG DATA: 700 QUESTIONS - VOLUME 4.

It deals with the requirements for Big Data management, the data structures used, the architecture and storage layers, Business Intelligence in the context of Big Data, and application virtualization.

5   BIG DATA: 700 QUESTIONS - VOLUME 5.

The book deals with SAAS, IAAS AND PAAS, Big Data implementation, overhead and hidden costs, Big Data for small businesses, digital security and data warehousing in the context of Big Data.

20.2.7 BIG DATA GLOSSARY.

Essential work to understand and master the Big Data universe, offering practical clarity on fundamental technical terms. With objective definitions, real-world examples, and intuitive organization, this glossary makes it easy to turn complex concepts into strategic insights.

Ideal for developers, data engineers, managers, and the curious who want to explore the transformative potential of data, quickly elevating your understanding and making you more competitive in an increasingly information-driven market.

21 Discover the "Artificial Intelligence and the Power of Data" Collection – An Invitation to Transform Your Career and Knowledge.

The "Artificial Intelligence and the Power of Data" Collection was created for those who want not only to understand Artificial Intelligence (AI), but also to apply it strategically and practically.

In a series of carefully crafted volumes, I unravel complex concepts in a clear and accessible manner, ensuring the reader has a thorough understanding of AI and its impact on modern societies.

No matter what your level of familiarity with the topic, this collection turns the difficult into the didactic, the theoretical into the applicable, and the technical into something powerful for your career.

21.1   Why buy this collection?

We are living through an unprecedented technological revolution, where AI is the driving force in areas such as medicine, finance, education, government, and entertainment.

The collection "Artificial Intelligence and the Power of Data" dives deep into all these sectors, with practical examples and reflections that go far beyond traditional concepts.

You'll find both the technical expertise and the ethical and social implications of AI encouraging you to see this technology not just as a tool, but as a true agent of transformation.

Each volume is a fundamental piece of this innovative puzzle: from machine learning to data governance and from ethics to practical application.

With the guidance of an experienced author who combines academic research with years of hands-on practice, this collection is more than a set of books – it's an indispensable guide for anyone looking to navigate and excel in this burgeoning field.

21.2   Who is this Collection for?

This collection is for everyone who wants to play a prominent role in the age of AI:

✓ Tech Professionals: Receive deep technical insights to expand their skills.

✓ Students and the Curious: have access to clear explanations that facilitate the understanding of the complex universe of AI.

✓ Managers, business leaders, and policymakers will also benefit from the strategic vision on AI, which is essential for making well-informed decisions.

✓ Professionals in Career Transition: Professionals in career transition or interested in specializing in AI will find here complete material to build their learning trajectory.

21.3   Much More Than Technique – A Complete Transformation.

This collection is not just a series of technical books; It is a tool for intellectual and professional growth.

With it, you go far beyond theory: each volume invites you to a deep reflection on the future of humanity in a world where machines and algorithms are increasingly present.

Be a leader in your industry, master the skills the market demands, and prepare for the future with the "Artificial Intelligence and the Power of Data" collection.

22 The Books of the Collection.

22.1 DATA, INFORMATION AND KNOWLEDGE IN THE AGE OF ARTIFICIAL INTELLIGENCE.

This book essentially explores the theoretical and practical foundations of Artificial Intelligence, from data collection to its transformation into intelligence. It focuses primarily on machine learning, AI training, and neural networks.

22.2 FROM DATA TO GOLD: HOW TO TURN INFORMATION INTO WISDOM IN THE AGE OF AI.

This book offers critical analysis on the evolution of Artificial Intelligence, from raw data to the creation of artificial wisdom, integrating neural networks, deep learning, and knowledge modeling.

It presents practical examples in health, finance, and education, and addresses ethical and technical challenges.

22.3 CHALLENGES AND LIMITATIONS OF DATA IN AI.

The book offers an in-depth analysis of the role of data in the development of AI exploring topics such as quality, bias, privacy, security, and scalability with practical case studies in healthcare, finance, and public safety.

22.4 HISTORICAL DATA IN DATABASES FOR AI: STRUCTURES, PRESERVATION AND PURGE.

This book investigates how historical data management is essential to the success of AI projects. It addresses the relevance of ISO standards to ensure quality and safety, in addition to analyzing trends and innovations in data processing.

22.5 CONTROLLED VOCABULARY FOR DATA DICTIONARY: A COMPLETE GUIDE.

This comprehensive guide explores the advantages and challenges of implementing controlled vocabularies in the context of AI and information science. With a detailed approach, it covers everything from the naming of data elements to the interactions between semantics and cognition.

22.6 DATA CURATION AND STEWARDSHIP FOR THE AI ERA.

This book presents advanced strategies for transforming raw data into valuable insights, with a focus on meticulous curation and efficient data management. In addition to technical solutions, it addresses ethical and legal issues, empowering the reader to face the complex challenges of information.

22.7 INFORMATION ARCHITECTURE.

The book addresses data management in the digital age, combining theory and practice to create efficient and scalable AI systems, with insights into modeling and ethical and legal challenges.

22.8 FUNDAMENTALS: THE ESSENTIALS TO MASTER ARTIFICIAL INTELLIGENCE.

An essential work for anyone who wants to master the key concepts of AI, with an accessible approach and practical examples.

The book explores innovations such as Machine Learning and Natural Language Processing, as well as ethical and legal challenges, and offers a clear view of the impact of AI on various industries.

22.9 LLMS - LARGE-SCALE LANGUAGE MODELS.

This essential guide helps you understand the revolution of Large-Scale Language Models (LLMs) in AI.

The book explores the evolution of GPTs and the latest innovations in human-computer interaction, offering practical insights into their impact on industries such as healthcare, education, and finance.

22.10 MACHINE LEARNING: FUNDAMENTALS AND ADVANCES.

This book offers a comprehensive overview of supervised and unsupervised algorithms, deep neural networks, and federated learning. In addition to addressing issues of ethics and explainability of models.

22.11 INSIDE SYNTHETIC MINDS.

This book reveals how these 'synthetic minds' are redefining creativity, work, and human interactions. This work presents a detailed analysis of the challenges and opportunities provided by these technologies, exploring their profound impact on society.

22.12 THE ISSUE OF COPYRIGHT.

This book invites the reader to explore the future of creativity in a world where human-machine collaboration is a reality, addressing questions about authorship, originality, and intellectual property in the age of generative AIs.

22.13 1121 QUESTIONS AND ANSWERS: FROM BASIC TO COMPLEX – PART 1 TO 4.

Organized into four volumes, these questions serve as essential practical guides to mastering key AI concepts.

Part 1 addresses information, data, geoprocessing, the evolution of artificial intelligence, its historical milestones and basic concepts.

Part 2 delves into complex concepts such as machine learning, natural language processing, computer vision, robotics, and decision algorithms.

Part 3 addresses issues such as data privacy, work automation, and the impact of large-scale language models (LLMs).

Part 4 explores the central role of data in the age of artificial intelligence, delving into the fundamentals of AI and its applications in areas such as mental health, government, and anti-corruption.

22.14 THE DEFINITIVE GLOSSARY OF ARTIFICIAL INTELLIGENCE.

This glossary presents more than a thousand artificial intelligence concepts clearly explained, covering topics such as Machine Learning, Natural Language Processing, Computer Vision, and AI Ethics.

- Part 1 contemplates concepts starting with the letters A to D.
- Part 2 contemplates concepts initiated by the letters E to M.
- Part 3 contemplates concepts starting with the letters N to Z.

22.15 PROMPT ENGINEERING - VOLUMES 1 TO 6.

This collection covers all the fundamentals of prompt engineering, providing a complete foundation for professional development.

With a rich variety of prompts for areas such as leadership, digital marketing, and information technology, it offers practical examples to improve clarity, decision-making, and gain valuable insights.

The volumes cover the following subjects:

- Volume 1: Fundamentals. Structuring Concepts and History of Prompt Engineering.
- Volume 2: Security and Privacy in AI.
- Volume 3: Language Models, Tokenization, and Training Methods.
- Volume 4: How to Ask Right Questions.
- Volume 5: Case Studies and Errors.
- Volume 6: The Best Prompts.

22.16   GUIDE TO BEING A PROMPT ENGINEER – VOLUMES 1 AND 2.

The collection explores the advanced fundamentals and skills required to be a successful prompt engineer, highlighting the benefits, risks, and the critical role this role plays in the development of artificial intelligence.

Volume 1 covers crafting effective prompts, while Volume 2 is a guide to understanding and applying the fundamentals of Prompt Engineering.

22.17   DATA GOVERNANCE WITH AI – VOLUMES 1 TO 3.

Find out how to implement effective data governance with this comprehensive collection. Offering practical guidance, this collection covers everything from data architecture and organization to protection and quality assurance, providing a complete view to transform data into strategic assets.

Volume 1 addresses practices and regulations. Volume 2 explores in depth the processes, techniques, and best practices for conducting effective audits on data models. Volume 3 is your definitive guide to deploying data governance with AI.

22.18   ALGORITHM GOVERNANCE.

This book looks at the impact of algorithms on society, exploring their foundations and addressing ethical and regulatory issues. It addresses transparency, accountability, and bias, with practical solutions for auditing and monitoring algorithms in sectors such as finance, health, and education.

22.19 FROM IT PRO TO AI EXPERT: THE ULTIMATE GUIDE TO A SUCCESSFUL CAREER TRANSITION.

For Information Technology professionals, the transition to AI represents a unique opportunity to enhance skills and contribute to the development of innovative solutions that shape the future.

In this book, we investigate the reasons for making this transition, the essential skills, the best learning path, and the prospects for the future of the IT job market.

22.20 INTELLIGENT LEADERSHIP WITH AI: TRANSFORM YOUR TEAM AND DRIVE RESULTS.

This book reveals how artificial intelligence can revolutionize team management and maximize organizational performance.

By combining traditional leadership techniques with AI-powered insights, such as predictive analytics-based leadership, you'll learn how to optimize processes, make more strategic decisions, and create more efficient and engaged teams.

22.21 IMPACTS AND TRANSFORMATIONS: COMPLETE COLLECTION.

This collection offers a comprehensive and multifaceted analysis of the transformations brought about by Artificial Intelligence in contemporary society.

- Volume 1: Challenges and Solutions in the Detection of Texts Generated by Artificial Intelligence.
- Volume 2: The Age of Filter Bubbles. Artificial Intelligence and the Illusion of Freedom.
- Volume 3: Content Creation with AI - How to Do It?
- Volume 4: The Singularity Is Closer Than You Think.
- Volume 5: Human Stupidity versus Artificial Intelligence.
- Volume 6: The Age of Stupidity! A Cult of Stupidity?

- Volume 7: Autonomy in Motion: The Intelligent Vehicle Revolution.
- Volume 8: Poiesis and Creativity with AI.
- Volume 9: Perfect Duo: AI + Automation.
- Volume 10: Who Holds the Power of Data?

22.22 BIG DATA WITH AI: COMPLETE COLLECTION.

The collection covers everything from the technological fundamentals and architecture of Big Data to the administration and glossary of essential technical terms.

The collection also discusses the future of humanity's relationship with the enormous volume of data generated in the databases of training in Big Data structuring.

- Volume 1: Fundamentals.
- Volume 2: Architecture.
- Volume 3: Implementation.
- Volume 4: Administration.
- Volume 5: Essential Themes and Definitions.
- Volume 6: Data Warehouse, Big Data, and AI.

23 About the Author.

I'm Marcus Pinto, better known as Prof. Marcão, a specialist in information technology, information architecture and artificial intelligence.

With more than four decades of dedicated work and research, I have built a solid and recognized trajectory, always focused on making technical knowledge accessible and applicable to all those who seek to understand and stand out in this transformative field.

My experience spans strategic consulting, education and authorship, as well as an extensive performance as an information architecture analyst.

This experience enables me to offer innovative solutions adapted to the constantly evolving needs of the technological market, anticipating trends and creating bridges between technical knowledge and practical impact.

Over the years, I have developed comprehensive and in-depth expertise in data, artificial intelligence, and information governance – areas that have become essential for building robust and secure systems capable of handling the vast volume of data that shapes today's world.

My book collection, available on Amazon, reflects this expertise, addressing topics such as Data Governance, Big Data, and Artificial Intelligence with a clear focus on practical applications and strategic vision.

Author of more than 150 books, I investigate the impact of artificial intelligence in multiple spheres, exploring everything from its technical bases to the ethical issues that become increasingly urgent with the adoption of this technology on a large scale.

In my lectures and mentorships, I share not only the value of AI, but also the challenges and responsibilities that come with its implementation – elements that I consider essential for ethical and conscious adoption.

I believe that technological evolution is an inevitable path. My books are a proposed guide on this path, offering deep and accessible insights for those who want not only to understand, but to master the technologies of the future.

With a focus on education and human development, I invite you to join me on this transformative journey, exploring the possibilities and challenges that this digital age has in store for us.

24 How to Contact Prof. Marcão.

24.1   For lectures, training and business mentoring.

marcao.tecno@gmail.com

24.2   Prof. Marcão, on Linkedin.

https://bit.ly/linkedin_profmarcao

www.ingramcontent.com/pod-product-compliance
Lightning Source LLC
La Vergne TN
LVHW022348060326
832902LV00022B/4312